Christabel Rose Coleridge

Hugh Crichton's Romance

Vol. 3

Christabel Rose Coleridge

Hugh Crichton's Romance
Vol. 3

ISBN/EAN: 9783337345433

Printed in Europe, USA, Canada, Australia, Japan

Cover: Foto ©Thomas Meinert / pixelio.de

More available books at **www.hansebooks.com**

HUGH CRICHTON'S ROMANCE

BY

CHRISTABEL R. COLERIDGE

AUTHOR OF 'LADY BETTY'

𝔍𝔬𝔟𝔢 𝔦𝔰 𝔞 𝔓𝔯𝔢𝔰𝔢𝔫𝔱 𝔣𝔬𝔯 𝔞 𝔐𝔦𝔤𝔥𝔱𝔶 𝔎𝔦𝔫𝔤

IN THREE VOLUMES

VOL. III.

London

MACMILLAN AND CO.

1875

CONTENTS

OF

THE THIRD VOLUME.

PART V.—*continued.*

CHAP.		PAGE
XXXI.	BEGINNING AFRESH . .	3
XXXII.	FAINT-HEARTED . .	21
XXXIII.	PIN-PRICKS .	39
XXXIV.	DIVIDED . .	59
XXXV.	MR. BLANDFORD OF FORDHAM	76
XXXVI.	AMONG THE PRIMROSES	96

PART VI.

AT THE YEAR'S END.

XXXVII.	ANOTHER CHANCE . . .	119
XXXVIII.	JEM'S IDEAL	135
XXXIX.	PAST AND PRESENT . .	153

CHAP.   PAGE

XL. PERPLEXITIES   .   .   .   171

XLI. THUNDER-SHOWERS .   .   191

XLII. THE MEETING OF THE WATERS .   214

XLIII. THE LESSON OF LOVE   .   .   230

XLIV. THE LESSON OF LIFE   .   .   248

PART V.—*continued.*

CHAPTER XXXI.

BEGINNING AFRESH.

'When all the world is old, lad,
    And all the trees are brown,
And all the sport is stale, lad,
    And all the wheels run down.'

It was on a soft mild afternoon early in February that Arthur came home—an afternoon with a pearly sky and gleams of pale spring sunshine to light the starry celandines and budding palms. Spring was coming—there were lambs in the meadows, and birds in the hedges, the gaily-painted barges floated down the slow water, children and young ladies tripped along the path—nothing was changed. Redhurst, always a cheerful place, was at its brightest, fresh and spring-like, yet

B 2

familiar as the golden crocuses in the garden-beds.

Mrs. Crichton was glad of the sunshine. Though rarely nervous she longed for the arrival to be over, and sent her young ladies to meet Frederica as she came from school, so that there was no one to receive her nephew but herself, arrayed in mourning, purposely lightened before his return. She heard him ring the bell, perhaps for the first time in his life, and came out to meet him.

'Well, my dear boy, I hardly expected you so soon; come in—I'm glad to see you.'

Arthur kissed her warmly, and followed her into the drawing-room.

'I think the train was punctual,' he said.

'Are you tired—did you stop in London?'

'Oh, yes, and I saw Jem. He says he will run down soon. I crossed yesterday, so I have had nothing of a journey to-day.'

'And—are you quite well, my dear?'

Mrs. Crichton did not mean to make much of the meeting; but she put her hand on his arm and looked at him tenderly, hardly able to speak. Arthur smiled a little.

'Very well,' he said, 'and glad to see you.'

Arthur was quite quiet and calm; but he was very grave, and made no attempt to feign an ordinary tone of feeling that could not have been real; he was always entirely genuine, and rarely thought of the effect of his own demeanour. Mrs. Crichton looked at him anxiously. He was a good deal tanned and rather thinner than of old; but she thought that he did look well and wonderfully like himself.

'Isn't Freddie here?' he said.

'Yes—there she is—she has been at school.'

Ah! He went forward rather eagerly to meet her; but Frederica, nervous and excited, and by no means sharing his absence

of self-consciousness, kissed him rather
boisterously than tenderly, and began to talk
fast because she was afraid of crying.

'I suppose Hugh is at the Bank,' said
Arthur ; but as he spoke there was a rush
and a scamper through the hall, and Snap,
his terrier, rushed upon him with a welcome
in which there was no cloud of embarrass
ment, and no room for regrets. After that
Arthur was glad to get away to look after
his luggage, and when he came back afternoon tea was in progress, and he sat down
and talked about his journey and the won-
ders of Rome, and the new coloured curtains
Jem had hung up in his highly-decorated
rooms. Arthur was a pleasant talker, and
they thought how nice it was to have him at
home again. But he looked vaguely about
the room betweenwhiles, as if its changes
perplexed him. He walked over to the
window and looked out, where the light was
dying away on the garden-paths. He had

expected to feel the first sight of home severely—he hardly felt anything except that he had been there for a long time—an interminable number of hours.

Hugh was, perhaps purposely, late, and at length Mrs. Crichton proposed going to dress, audibly wondering why he did not come.

'There he is!' said Freddie, as a horse's hoofs sounded. 'Hugh,' she added, throwing open the door, 'here's Arthur!'

Arthur started up and went forward.

'Hugh!' he said with a sort of eagerness:

'Well, Arthur, how d'ye do?' but as Hugh uttered this commonplace greeting his hand was as cold as ice. They exchanged half-a-dozen words as to Arthur's journey and the weather, and separated in two minutes to dress; and the much-dreaded meeting was over.

Everyone was eager to talk at dinner,

and a little bit afraid of home topics, and
soon Frederica started what she conceived
to be a delightfully safe and interesting subject.

'Oh, Arthur, we have heard of you
lately from someone you met in Italy.'

'Really; who is that?'

'Why, a young lady who teaches us
Italian—she was at a place called Caletto——'

'Miss Rosa Mattei?' said Arthur. 'Has
she come here?'

'No—it is her sister. Oh, she is the
dearest little thing—her name is Violante—
do you remember?'

'Violante! You don't say so! I remember her perfectly. Is she at Miss Venning's? Well, that is the most extraordinary
chance!' exclaimed Arthur, much interested.
'I never thought she would really go to
school!'

'Oh, yes; Miss Venning knows her aunt,
I believe.'

'Poor little thing!' said Arthur. 'I was so sorry for her. She—she lost her voice, you know.'

'Oh, yes, I know all about it. Flossy told me. She likes being at school much better than on the stage.'

'They were very kind to me. It was like a bit of a romance. She used to ask me questions about England. Why, they don't make her teach, do they? What a shame!'

'Arthur, what nonsense!' cried his sister. 'But Violante just bewitches people.'

'Well! she doesn't look fit to fight her way. By the by, Hugh, Jem told me that you and he saw her act. It was rather a failure, wasn't it?'

As no one had expected Hugh to take any particular interest in this conversation his dead silence surprised no one. A great fern hid him from his mother, and no one else looked at or thought of him. He answered Arthur, mechanically:

' I believe it was considered so.'

' But was her voice so lovely?' said Freddie.

' They said so, I think.'

' Oh, Hugh!' said his mother, laughing, ' what opportunities you throw away. We must ask Jem, Arthur?'

' Ay, I should think Jem would have been enraptured. I thought of him when I saw her in the golden sunshine piling up the grapes, and they gave me coffee because I was tired and thirsty. I can't believe she could do anything so prosaic as teach.'

The subject in its various branches lasted for some time, and when the ladies went away Arthur continued it:

' I don't suppose Freddie *does* know all about her. You know she was engaged to the manager of the opera-house there, and he threw her over when she lost her voice. So the poor little thing was fretting her heart out.'

'How do you know?' said Hugh, with a sense of being suffocated.

'Oh, there was an old *cantatrice* who had charge of the sisters, and she used to talk to me. And one could see the poor child was unhappy—indeed, she owned as much.'

'She would be quite pleased to see you again.'

'Well, I daresay she would,' said Arthur, carelessly; 'but I don't suppose Miss Venning would allow—' He stopped, as the words suggested a different recollection, and after a moment went on, gravely:

'Hugh, I don't want to lose any more time. You will let me begin work to-morrow?'

'If you wish it,' said Hugh, without looking at him. 'You can do as you wish always.'

'Thanks; you're very good, Hugh. I'll do my best. You'll be patient?'

Poor boy, he was naturally outspoken, and wanted, perhaps, a word of sympathy and support in this painful home-coming; but Hugh only answered, as they left the room: 'I could not be otherwise,' and the coldness of the tone neutralised the kindness of the words. He lingered behind as Arthur turned towards the drawing-room, and went into his study. He would not have believed beforehand how little he would have thought about his cousin on that first day of meeting, which he had dreaded so much beforehand. His cold, short answers had come, not from embarrassment, but because he was wholly absorbed in something else. Had he avoided Violante to find her close at his side? Had he really passed her every morning and evening? Ah—and the violets—he had thrown them away! Perhaps this fact gave to the sensible Mr. Spencer Crichton the keenest sense of lost opportunity that he had ever experienced. She had not, then, for-

gotten him. Had she come there knowing
of his neighbourhood? Or had she really
never cared for him at all? Arthur confirmed her engagement to the manager, and
seemed well-informed, much *too* well informed as to her sentiments with regard to
the breach of it. Hugh was not naturally
trustful, and through all his passion he had
never trusted Violante, never forgotten that
she was a foreigner and of altogether different
training from his own. Besides, she *had*
been false to him. He had seen her with
the diamonds on her neck—he had been
deceived by her confiding softness—hadn't
she been just as ready to tell her troubles to
Arthur as to himself? At home Hugh was
much more convinced of the unsuitableness
of his choice than he had been in Italy; and
now, after all that had passed, what right had
he to create such a family convulsion as
would be caused by any renewal of it? His
love remained, but the charm of it seemed to

have faded. The bitter hours he had lately
passed had half awakened him from his daz-
zling holiday dream, taking from it the force
it might else have had to bend his pride to
own what had been passing in his mind all
the summer, and to shake the conviction that
had a sort of uncomfortable attraction to
him—that he had lost the right to choose
his own happiness against the pleasure of
his family. How could he say to his mother
now, ' Consent to this—I cannot live without
her'—when, through him, Arthur must live
without his love? To do so he must have
been careless and selfish—and Hugh was
neither, in intention, or he must have been
able to sound the depths and rise to the
height of a humility of which he could not
even conceive. Besides, this unlucky love
paid the penalty of all feelings that are un-
likely and, as it were, against the nature and
the circumstances of those who experience
them. It was sweet and enticing, but it

was insecure and beset by doubts and
misgivings.

But yet, when he and Arthur rode away
together the next morning, Hugh's sense of
being alone with his cousin was lost in the
knowledge that he must pass Oxley Manor.
He looked up at it, and his heart thrilled;
but no face was at the window, no violets,
cool and fragrant, touched his hand. Where
was she? What was she doing? He was
absorbed in the present, full of an excitement
which enraged him, but which made life
worth having after all. Arthur, by his side,
had his own vision, but it was back in the
past. Those walls held no imprisoned
princess for him. That little green gate
could never open again and show her standing under the ivy, with her happy eyes and
brisk light tread. During his long absence
Arthur had felt continuously that he had
lost Mysie; he began now to realise that the
world was going on without her. He found

the home life hard. He had never expected
to be other than sad ; but he had not fore-
seen that one thing would be worse than
another, that there would be some paths
that he dared not tread, some faces that he
could not bear to see. When, as he strolled
through the garden after breakfast, he suddenly felt that he *could* not turn down the
path towards the river, when he counted with
nervous dread each familiar object yet to be
met, he was surprised and vexed with himself. He had thought that everything that
recalled his darling must be sweet : what was
the meaning of this horror which he tried to
forget in taking part in the family talk and
life around him ; when his natural cheerfulness asserted itself, and Hugh looked at him
with wonder? And then, when he fancied
that he should rather like some occupation
or amusement, why did he suddenly break
down in the attempt to share in it, and only
long to get away by himself? Even his work

at the Bank—which was less trying, since it was entirely new—was sometimes a great burden to him after his long desultoriness; but in this case there was something definite to struggle with, and he could succeed in conquering himself; but at home he could not tell what was the matter with him, and no one helped him to find out—his aunt continuously ignoring his fluctuating spirits, and congratulating herself when he was lively and talkative; while Hugh, seeing that the cheerfulness was spontaneous when it came, marvelled at it, and, while he could not bear to see him dispirited, wondered what his world would think if he showed his moods so plainly. Nevertheless, he was not always even-tempered, and, as Arthur had lost his careless good-humour, Hugh would be shocked to find himself arguing hotly or speaking sharply to one with whom he was bound to have entire patience; and Arthur would wonder why, with such a weight at

his heart, things should seem all out of joint
—not because Mysie was dead—but because
Hugh frowned, or Freddie laughed, or some
trifle put him out of his way. He had returned home on a Tuesday, and by the end
of the week had grown fairly perplexed with
himself. On the Saturday afternoon, however, he walked out early from Oxley by
himself, and, taking a roundabout way
through some of the woods belonging to
Ashenfold, felt soothed and cheered by the
pleasant light and air of the early spring.
When he was thus alone, and could let quiet
thoughts of Mysie have their way unchecked
and undisturbed, he lost the sense of discord
and trouble ; and, as was, perhaps, too much
his wont, the sensations of the hour obli-
terated all others, and he stood leaning over
a gate, watching the faint, pinky tints on the
woods, and listening to a robin singing close
at hand. Suddenly, in the copse beside him,
there was a sharp noise—the report of a gun.

Arthur started, as if he had been shot him-self, his heart beat violently; he caught at the gate, and held it hard; the sound struck his ears like a repetition of that one fatal shot. It was some minutes before he reco-vered himself sufficiently to be conscious of anything but his own sensations, and when he looked up at last and drew breath he was fairly exhausted. He had thought so little of himself, and so much of his sorrow, that he had had no conception how severe the shock to his nerves had been. He was annoyed with himself and very thankful that no one had been there to see, so that he care-fully concealed the incident from everybody; but it set him on the look-out, as it were, for his own feelings; and, while it certainly roused him to attempt to conceal them, he so dreaded a recurrence of the shock, and was so ignorant as to what might cause it, that he shrank from many old associations which he had previously never thought of avoiding.

The sound rang in his ears, and he tried
vehemently to distract his mind from it by
talking and laughing with his aunt's guests;
and when Hugh saw him playing bezique
he wondered whether he was to envy him
for heroic self-control or for boyish careless-
ness and reaction.

CHAPTER XXXII.

FAINT-HEARTED.

' The grave of all things hath its violet.'

THE Redhurst drawing-room was looking
uncommonly cheerful on the Saturday week
after Arthur's return ; and Jem, recently
arrived, was enjoying an unwonted *tête-à-tête*
with his mother. It would be, perhaps, untrue
to say that a person with affections so even
as Mrs. Crichton's had a favourite son ; but
there was much in Jem's ways that suited
her, and he had the charm of novelty. He
was strolling about the room, criticizing the
alterations somewhat unfavourably.

'I say, mamma, what did you buy this

thing for?' touching the chintz. 'I could
have chosen you a much better one. Why
didn't you write to me?'

'Really, my dear, I didn't think of asking
you to choose my drawing-room furniture.
Why don't you like it?'

'Why don't I like it? Why, it's altogether incorrect. Those autumn leaves are
false art.'

'Dear me, don't you like my leaves?'
They're so natural you might sweep them
up.'

'Exactly. You might as well be out in
the garden. Now, there's a thing up in one
of the spare bed-rooms. It's yellow, with a
faint brown pattern——'

'*That*, Jem! Why, it belonged to your
grandmother Spencer, and was moved here
when she came and spent her last year with
us. It's hideous. I was going to have it
taken down.'

'It's about the best thing in the house,'

said Jem, critically. 'You should have it made up for this room.'

'Ah, my dear fellow, I hope your wife will have some taste of her own.'

'I hope she'll leave it to me. I shall stipulate she does when I marry and settle.'

'I am afraid, my dear, life in London doesn't lead young men to marry and settle.'

'Well, mamma, I'm sure I don't know about that,' said Jem, sitting down on the obnoxious chintz and stroking his beard. 'Girls look out for so much now-a-days.'

'I hope, my dear, you haven't been falling in with any girl,' said Mrs. Crichton, composedly—for she was not excitable—but a little struck by Jem's manner. 'You make so many acquaintances. When you were abroad I was quite anxious.'

'I assure you, mamma, *I* was a miracle of discretion when I was abroad—couldn't have been better with you at my elbow,' said Jem, unable to resist a little emphasis.

'Well, I am sure, I wonder you did not make a heroine of that little Italian girl, Arthur's acquaintance. Hugh said you met her.'

'Hugh said I met her!' ejaculated Jem, 'Well, if that isn't cool!'

'Why, something was said of seeing her act, and, of course, my dear boy, I didn't suppose *Hugh* had been the one to discover her merits.'

'I assure you, mother, I was quite as discreet as Arthur or Hugh either. But what made Mademoiselle Mattei a subject of conversation?'

'Why, she is at Miss Venning's at school.'

'Good heavens!' ejaculated Jem, utterly off his guard; then, catching himself up: '*At school!* Extraordinary!'

'Yes, but I believe there's nothing extraordinary about her. So pray, my dear, don't go and do anything foolish.'

'Why am I always to be the black

sheep?' said Jem, in an injured tone, but with inward laughter. 'Hugh and Arthur saw *quite* as much of her as I did.'

'Well, we may put poor Arthur out of the question, and as for Hugh, do you think I've any reason to be anxious in that way about him?'

'So you wouldn't like an Italian daughter-in-law?'

'My dear, don't be absurd,' said Mrs. Crichton, contemplating her wool-work. 'How can you talk of such a thing? I should like to see both you and Hugh married, but I dread your doing something foolish when I think of the number of times you have been on the verge of it—and as for Hugh——'

'Well, as for Hugh?'

'I really despair of his ever turning his thoughts in that direction.'

'How are you all getting along together?' said Jem, rather glad to change the conversation.

'Oh, pretty well,' said Mrs. Crichton, sighing. 'Of course, Arthur, poor dear boy, has ups and downs; but he is very cheerful, in and out, and I make a point of going on as usual.'

'And he and Hugh get on comfortably?'

'Yes. I tell Hugh it is absurd to expect that he should not flag sometimes. Now, Sunday was a trial. He went to church in the morning, but he was more knocked up afterwards than I have seen him at all; but the next day he was quite ready to be interested in these pleasant Dysarts who have come to Ashenfold. Hugh was quite angry with me for making him come in to see them; but we can't shut ourselves up, and I must ask them to dinner in a quiet way. It is much better for Arthur. Then, there was another thing. I wanted him to come to the Rectory with me—to get it over, you know—but Hugh interfered, and said no one should urge him to make such an effort, in such a peremptory way I had to give it up.'

'I should avoid discussions,' said James. 'It's hard work for them both. By the way, mamma,' he added, having conducted the conversation well away from its former matrimonial channel, 'do you know that there is going to be a great choir festival at H——, in the cathedral in Easter week— shall you go?'

'Is there? Oh, no, I hadn't thought of it.'

'I expect it will be rather fine. I shall run down, and if you did care about taking Freddie I daresay the Haywards would get you good places.'

'The Haywards?'

'The Archdeacon, you know. He is a Canon of H——. Young Hayward's in the War Office. I know him. There are some daughters.'

'Oh, I know Mrs. Hayward very well. She was at the only ball to which I ever took

dear Mysie at H——, with her daughters;
tall, fine girls, rather insipid.'

'They're very superior,' said Jem, in an
odd, meek voice; but, as he was not much in
the habit of admiring superior young ladies,
his mother only said:

'Are they? Their mother is a very lady-
like woman. Well, I should not mind going
over if Freddie wished it. I daresay Flossy
Venning might like to go with us.'

'Oh, thank you,' began Jem. 'I mean
the organist is a friend of mine. Oh, there's
Hugh. How d'ye do?'

'I didn't know you were here, Jem,' said
Hugh, as he came into the room.

'I came by the early train. Where's
Arthur?'

'He preferred walking. How long shall
you be here, Jem?'

'Till Tuesday.'

'Oh, then,' said Mrs. Crichton, 'Hugh, I
think I shall ask the Dysarts to excuse a short

notice and come here quite quietly on Monday night. As it is Lent, that is a reason for having no party.'

' There can be no reason wanted for that,' interrupted Hugh. 'Mother, how can you think of such a thing? It is not suitable, and must be intolerable to Arthur.'

' Really, Hugh,' said his mother, for once offended, ' I am the best judge of what is suitable. You talk as if I wished to give a ball; and Arthur does not dislike a little society.'

' If he does not'—said Hugh, and then broke off, ' Perhaps he does not.'

' Why don't you ask him?' suggested James.

' Because he has never shown any of this foolish reluctance,' said Mrs. Crichton; ' and, indeed, my dear, I can't give into you about it.'

She rose and went away as she spoke, and James said :

'How's this, Hugh? Things going all crooked?'

'Of course they are,' said Hugh, bitterly. 'How could they go right? As for Arthur, I don't profess to understand him. I daresay he does like amusement, but he can't bear this place. How they can say he is less altered than they expected! I can feel the chance allusions stab him!'

'Then do you think he is putting a great force on himself?'

'No, no,' said Hugh, in an odd, restless tone. 'It's just as it comes, I believe. But they say he bears it beautifully, because his spirits come back in and out. He is boyish enough still. I daresay in a year's time it will all be pretty well over.'

'It strikes me, Hugh, you are more out of sorts than Arthur.'

'I?' said Hugh. 'If Arthur feels one half—No, he could not choose to be always with me.'

Hugh knitted his brows and walked over to the window. His was the perplexity of an erring, earnest nature watching another live over a difficult piece of life, by means of a more gracious temperament, succeeding, as he felt, without the struggles that went towards his own failures. Arthur behaved much better to him than he did to Arthur, but he did not take half so much pains about it. This is always an unsatisfactory consciousness, and in Hugh's case it was intensified by the morbid interest that he was forced to take in his cousin.

'Mother's been telling me all the news,' said James, to change the subject.

Hugh understood his marked tone at once.

'Remember, Jem, that is closed for ever,' he said. 'If you breathe one word of the past, in joke or earnest, to my mother or Arthur, it will be past forgiveness.'

'I'm sure I don't want to stir it up,' said Jem; 'but it is a strange turn of fate.'

'It will make no difference,' said Hugh, in a tone that meant 'it *shall* not.'

James was silent. Hugh's resolve was exactly what he had always counselled him to make, yet he could not help thinking of Violante's look of joy at seeing him, and wondering whether that light was quenched in her soft eyes for ever.

In the meantime, Arthur had not taken his solitary walk without a purpose. However far Hugh might be right in supposing that he allowed his feelings to drift as they would, he was becoming conscious that there was some cowardice in shrinking from anything that could excite them. He must stand by Mysie's grave—and he must stand there alone; for on Sunday he had not dared to lift his eyes as he walked down the path. She was buried in a corner of the church-yard where it was especially green and still;

close by the wall of the Rectory garden, over which a bright pink almond-tree was visible. Snowdrops and violets were thrusting their heads through the short turf between the graves, and were blooming in sweet abundance round the white cross that marked where she lay, while several half-faded wreaths were placed above them. There was nothing here to make Arthur nervous, —he wondered why he had stayed away so long. He was full of grief, yet something of the peaceful spirit of the past came shining back into his heart as he knelt there in the spring sunshine, and kissed the letters of Mysie's name. It was better, he thought, than being far away. He had risen to his feet, and was still dreamily gazing, when he heard a startled step at his side, and, turning, saw Florence Venning, bright, tall, and blooming, with a basket of flowers in her hand.

'Flossy!'

'Oh, I did not see you—I—I'll go!' said Flossy, crimson with the sense of intrusion.

'No, don't go. I am very glad to see you,' he said, as he took her hand and held it, while they looked down at the grave together.

'Did you put these?' he said, touching the wreaths.

'Only this cross. The school-girls bring them on Sunday,' faltered Flossy, as she bent down and showed how the frame of the cross was made to hold water, which she now replenished from a little jug she had brought with her. Arthur, with a look of entreaty, and with trembling inapt fingers took the flowers and began to place them in the cross. Poor fellow, he did it very badly; but she refrained from helping him, and let him put the last snowdrop in himself.

'Flossy,' he said, suddenly, 'if I were lying there, and she were left, do you think she could have—have endured to live?'

'Yes, Arthur,' Flossy said, in her full tones, which vibrated with intense feeling, 'I think she could. I think she would have found a good life somehow; like—like a robin in the snow,' as one fluttered down beside them. 'She was so clear and real— I think she would.'

Arthur had sat down on a broad, flat stone near, still gazing at the flowers.

'She was not so weak,' he murmured.

'Oh, Arthur, you have not been weak. Everyone says——'

'No one knows,' he answered. 'All that should help me has no reality apart from *her*.'

'But it is not apart from her, Arthur,' said Flossy, earnestly. 'I——'

'Yes?' said Arthur, looking up.

'*Even* I,' said Flossy, humbly, 'I think of her at church, and doing my work, or on beautiful days like this.'

'Yes, dear Flossy, I'm sure you do,' said

Arthur, gratified; but not as if he took the words home.

'And I hope,' said Flossy, 'that it will make me a better girl, and more like her.'

'You are right, Flossy,' said Arthur, after a pause, with more spirit. 'I don't want to give up, and everyone is so kind to me; they all think of what I like. But,' he added, in a passionate undertone, 'she was my angel; and all prayers, Sundays, all the things that comfort a good girl like you, are filled with longing for her!'

'But they won't be less dear for that?' whispered Flossy.

'No,' he said, 'No, I'll hold on!'

And he felt then that through such holy associations his lost love might still be a star in his path, and lead him, not back to his old self, but on to something better, and even brighter. But, then, how could he tune his life to such a solemn melody as this? He longed for the joy-bells, and even the jingling tunes of his old, easy boyhood. He was so weary of his heavy heart. He knew, as Flossy could not know, why men plunged into folly, and even sin, to drown grief. He would not do that; but he thought how incredible it would have been to Flossy that there were times when he wanted to forget Mysie—times that came oftener as the months went by. He would have walked so contentedly on the easy, unheroic meadows of every-day life, and fate, or the hand of God, had forced him on to the rocky paths of sorrow. Just at that moment he caught a glimpse of the golden gate above them.

'How many birds there are here!' he said, after a silence.

'Do you know why? said Flossy. 'Mrs. Harcourt comes and feeds them here every morning and evening, because *she* was so fond of birds.'

'And I have never been to see her. I'll

go now,' said Arthur, rising with sudden
energy.

'I came from there,' said Flossy.   'This
is Mrs. Harcourt's jug.'

'Well, then, let us come,' he said, without giving himself time to hesitate, and
Florence took up her basket and followed
him into the garden.

CHAPTER XXXIII.

PIN-PRICKS.

'The mind has a thousand eyes,
And the heart but one.
But the light of a whole life dies
When love is done.'

THE Rectory drawing-room window was
open to the sunshine, and Mrs. Harcourt was
standing by it, waiting for Flossy. But
Arthur turned aside from it, and went round
to the door in front.

'Who is that, my dear?' said the old
lady, as Flossy ran up to her.

'It is Arthur,' she said. 'I met him
there. He said he ought to come and see
you.'

'Ah, poor boy, I'm glad,' said Mrs. Har-

court, as she went to let him in, while Flossy
exclaimed nervously :

'Oh, Violante, I forgot you. Never
mind, it will be just as well.'

'Is it Signor Arthur?' asked Violante,
who sometimes accompanied Miss Florence
on half-holiday walks, and had needed no
teaching to consider Redhurst sacred ground.

'Yes,' said Flossy, as Arthur and Mrs.
Harcourt came in. He looked very pale,
while Mrs. Harcourt, half-tearful, half-hospi-
table, was eagerly welcoming him.

'Ah, my dear Arthur, we have been
longing to see you; but I can't get out much
now; and I know—I know you could hardly
come. It is very good of you.'

'I am almost all day in Oxley,' he said ;
'but I hope you are well, and the Rector?'

'Pretty well, my dear, for our time of
life. We have had a lonely winter; but we
push along together, you see.'

Arthur managed to smile, but his face

went to Flossy's heart, though neither she nor Mrs. Harcourt knew exactly how the fifty years which the old husband and wife had 'had wi' ane anither' had once seemed to stretch before the young lovers, who never saw of them a single day.

'You have been getting some tea for us, Mrs. Harcourt?' she said.

'Oh, yes, my dear. Now, do you pour it out, and Arthur will have some. But will your young Italian friend drink tea?'

'Oh, yes, signora, I like tea,' and, with a start of relief, Arthur turned at the sound of her voice.

'Mademoiselle Mattei!' he said; 'I did not know you;' and, in truth, Violante was much altered at first sight by her dark winter dress and jacket, and little black hat with a red plume.

Arthur shook hands with her, and asked her how she liked England.

'I like it very much.'

' Why, we were very near an explanation. If you had told me where you were going to school I could have enlightened you much better as to what your life would be like there.'

' But I did not know myself,' said Violante, colouring as she thought of what a difference a few explanations might have made. 'I did not know anything,' and her sweet voice faltered with its weight of meaning.

' But I was right, wasn't I, when I gave you good advice? You have found——'

' Miss Florence,' said Violante, with a grateful look.

She felt as if Signor Arthur was quite an old friend. He had seen Rosa and her father, and she began to tell him about them, while Flossy made a few words of explanation to Mrs. Harcourt as to their previous meeting.

' I expect to find my cousin James at home,' he said. 'You remember him?'

'Yes, Arthur,' said Flossy. 'It's the strangest thing that she should have met you without knowing that Mr. Crichton and James were your cousins, and that then she should come here!'

'Mr. Hugh never comes to see me,' said Mrs. Harcourt.

'Doesn't he?' said Arthur. 'I will tell him that he should. There's the Rector.'

Mr. Harcourt, with more tact than his wife, only gave Arthur a warm handshake. Violante rose and curtsied to him in a pretty reverential fashion that pleased and touched him, and while he complimented her, in a little old-fashioned Italian, Flossy said aside:

'It makes Violante very shy to hear of anyone who saw her act; and, as Mary isn't very fond of the subject, we say very little about it.'

'Ah, yes, poor child! It's a mortifying recollection if she made a failure of it. She's a lovely creature. What on earth does she do with herself?'

'Oh, many things. Surely, Arthur, you don't think she need be useless because she's pretty?' and, in the little laugh that followed Flossy's return to her natural inclination for argument, Arthur took his leave.

It was a great relief to have got this afternoon's work over, and comfortable to find Jem at home when he got there, cheerful and chatty, and taking no apparent notice of his words or looks, yet with a little undercurrent of sympathy that he felt all the time. James amused everybody, and put them into good-humour, taking the burden of cheerfulness off their shoulders; and yet he avoided every word that could have touched painfully on his cousin or brother—or would have done so, had not some mention of a new opera recalled Violante to Arthur after dinner, when both he and Freddie demanded a description of her performances, as he stood on the hearthrug, looking round at his audience. Hugh was sitting on one side of the fire, holding up a 'Quarterly Review;' the ladies looked expectant over their work; and Arthur, leaning back in a low chair in front of him, was looking right up in his face.

'Well,' said Jem, apparently measuring his beard, hair by hair; 'I only saw her once. She acted badly and sang well, but it was a failure——'

'How so? She was enough applauded,' abruptly said Hugh; and then could have bitten his tongue out for speaking.

'She is pretty, you know,' said Jem.

'Lovely,' said Arthur. 'There's a sort of pathetic grace about her; but I suppose it didn't tell at a distance.'

It would be difficult to say whether their admiration, or the careless, critical tone in which it was uttered, enraged Hugh the most.

'Since her public career has ceased,' he
said, 'it seems a pity to discuss it.'

'Yes. It's hardly fair,' said Arthur;
'but she interested me, poor child, and I was
very glad to see her with Flossy. She is
sure to be well taken care of, and, perhaps,
she'll forget her troubles.'

'What troubles?' said Hugh, sternly.

'Why, I told you the other day,' said
Arthur, regardful of Frederica's presence.
'She looks twice as bright as she did in
Italy.'

'Now it seems to me,' said Mrs. Crichton,
'that you are all making a very unnecessary
talk about her. Miss Venning has decidedly
stretched a point in having her here. I
don't altogether approve of it. Young ladies
shouldn't have histories, and they should
keep her and hers in the background.'

'Aunt Lily, I think that would be mean,'
said Frederica.

'Aunt Lily's never seen her,' said Arthur.

'No, my dear, I don't feel any curiosity about her,' said Mrs. Crichton, didactically.

Jem—no other word will express it— giggled ; Hugh sprang to his feet, and, happily for the preservation of his secret, knocked over the lamp beside him, and in the confusion that followed Violante was forgotten, and he contrived to apologise and make his escape.

Such discussions rendered him furious, far more so than any amount of opposition could have done while he had had the one purpose of marrying Violante clear and straight before him. Then he would have borne patiently with his mother's natural opposition, and would have smiled at any- one else's. But now that they should all dare to praise her, and judge her, and ' take an interest' in her ! It made him very angry, and yet he was ashamed of his own con- nection with it. He would not have had it discovered for the world ; and then, when he

knew this feeling to be despicable, it was
justified by the knowledge of the pain and
disturbance any discovery would cause,
and increased by his jealousy of Violante's
reported confidences and conversations.
Arthur had been eager about nothing else.
Hugh had an unbounded belief in Violante's
irresistible charms, and none in the depth
and permanency of Arthur's sorrow, even
while that sorrow made his own. He was
never in the same mind for five minutes at a
time, angry, miserable, jealous, and self-
reproachful. He was sacrificing himself, of
course, in giving up all his chances of winning
her, and yet he could not quite rid himself
of the suspicion that he was false and cruel,
and that he had been his best self when he
defied the world for her sake. If accident
had thrown her in his way the whole current
of events might have been changed; but he
could not and would not seek her, though he
thought about her enough to make chance

allusions far more his dread than they ever were Arthur's, who never thought of them till they came ; and he bemoaned himself over the Dysart dinner-party, the announcement of which his cousin hardly heeded.

'Hugh has become exceedingly cross,' Freddie said to Jem, with the freedom of speech of the Redhurst household.

'Then, don't make him more so,' was Jem's advice, given with equal openness.

The party was merely to consist of Colonel and Mrs. Dysart, their two elder daughters, and one of their sons, who was discovered to be at home and invited at the last minute. It was difficult to see why a few extra people should make any difference, but Jem dressed himself with a sense of preparing to walk on egg-shells, and Arthur felt suddenly reluctant, and as if the sense of even this small festivity was depressing.

'My dear Jem,' his mother had said, 'I look to you to make it go off well.' But the

second Miss Dysart was very pretty, and just
in the style Jem admired, and he was
speedily absorbed in discussing a new novel
with her, and forgot to guide the rest of the
party, who talked of the neighbourhood and
the society in the manner of people enter-
taining new comers. The ladies of the
Dysart party were very conscious of the
recent history of their entertainers; and, perhaps, Miss Dysart was a little disappointed
that Arthur's manner and conversation were
so much like other people's. The gentlemen
were less well informed, or more forgetful;
and about half-way through dinner—after the
shops of Oxley, and the excellence of Miss
Venning's school for girls, and the doubtful
advantages of the grammar-school for boys,
had been well discussed—the inevitable subject of a country dinner-party made its
appearance, and young Dysart, across the
table, began to ask Arthur about the shooting. Hugh paused suddenly in what he was

saying, as Arthur answered: 'I am afraid you haven't much at Ashenfold; but ours is pretty good.'

'You shoot, I suppose?' said young Dysart.

'Oh, yes,' said Arthur, but with a catch in his breath.

'We shall take a day together, now and then, I hope, Mr. Crichton?' said Colonel Dysart to Hugh.

'No. I have given it up,' said Hugh, with sudden abrupt emphasis. 'I shall let my shooting.' He spoke as if he were confessing his faith on the scaffold; and, in the midst of the dead silence that ensued, James was heard wildly asking his little country-bred neighbour if she had ever been to a pigeon-match at Hurlingham; while Arthur, at the sound of his voice, said, with an effort that he could not conceal:

'The Ribstones are the great sportsmen in these parts. Sir William always has

plenty of pheasants;' and Mrs. Dysart caught
up the Hurlingham shuttlecock and conducted the conversation safely on to the
Princess of Wales. Arthur joined in, but
his eyes looked absent, and once or twice he
missed the answers to what he had said;
while Jem's pretty neighbour looked at him
with the tears in her eyes. No one could
forget what had passed ; and, indeed, in such
a household as Redhurst, this matter of the
shooting was a practical difficulty, and a
subject that could not be tabooed.

The guests had hardly departed when
Hugh said suddenly :

' To set this matter at rest for ever—as
long as I live I shall never touch a gun
again. Rest assured of it.'

No one answered, till Arthur said, moving
away :

' Good night, Aunt Lily, I'll go to bed.
I'm tired.'

Then James broke out :

'Really, Hugh, I am surprised at you!'

'Would you have me let anyone—would you have me let Arthur think that I could ever shoot again?'

'Who cares whether you do or not?' said Jem, angrily. 'Neither you nor Arthur can live without hearing the subject mentioned, and the only way is to pass it off quietly. He would have got over it in a minute if you had been silent, and next time it would have been a matter of course to him. Now you have raised up a scarecrow for ever.'

'Yes,' said Mrs. Crichton. 'It would be all very well to let the shooting for a time——'

'Of course, mother, I meant with your permission,' said Hugh, who was very punctilious as to invading his mother's rights.

'Nonsense, my dear. As if I should interfere with you about it! But now you have made our friends uncomfortable, and Arthur will feel the impossibility of it, instead of slipping back to it naturally by degrees. And you have made a most painful scene.' Here Mrs. Crichton herself ended in tears— half-nervous and half-sorrowful.

'It only shows,' said Hugh, passionately, 'that life here is impossible for Arthur and me. It is a problem that cannot be worked out. What is there left that has not that awful mark on it: the fields, the river—and would you have it supposed that I do not feel it?'

'I thought,' said James, drily, 'that it was Arthur's feelings, not yours, that were in question.'

Hugh paused, manifestly checked by this observation, and James went on: 'We all feel enough sorrow, but this is not a question of feelings but of nerves, as it seems to me. Arthur's are naturally strong, and these things may not affect him as they do you.'

'As to that,' said Hugh, 'one thing is as

bad as another. I have shirked no associations. They don't affect me.'

'Then, if not,' said his mother, 'why did
you speak as you did to-night?'

'Because I was thinking of him,' said
Hugh. 'Must I not feel them through him?
What would he think of me if I seemed not
to care? Am I not bound to spare him?'

'You set to work about it in a very odd
manner,' said James.

'My dear,' said Mrs. Crichton, 'it is what
I always told you. You will insist on looking
on this matter from a morbid point of view.
Just drop that, and time will heal all things
—even such grief as ours and poor Arthur's.
And I don't think he will feel these things
after the first. He never had any nerves, as
a boy, you know.'

'You cannot drop facts,' said Hugh,
wearily, 'but I have been wrong, as it seems,
somehow. There's no use in arguing
about it.'

'Yes, my dear, you were quite wrong,' said Mrs. Crichton, cheerfully, as he left the room ; ' so there's an end of it.'

Arthur, meanwhile, was reflecting on the practical aspect of the case. Although Redhurst was not a household where sport was made the business of life, it was one into the ordinary habits of which it entered considerably; and, perhaps, from his connection with the town, Hugh was a little tenacious of this privilege of the county. He liked sporting matters to be well managed, and Arthur was a very good shot and genuinely fond of the pursuit. He really could not conceive how the civilities of life could go on, or the ordinary intercourse with their neighbours be maintained, as the year went round, without it. Certainly, they must see and hear of it, if they declined to join in it themselves. Arthur had formed no resolutions about it; and, but for his experience in the Ashenfold woods, would have been

ready to take it up by degrees, with a heavy
heart enough and with little interest, but as
part of the life he had got to struggle back
to. And, surely, that would never happen to
him again. Arthur was much more ready
to resist these involuntary sensations than the
listlessness and dejection that seemed to have
become natural to him. Hugh's speech had,
of course, been intensely painful; but without
it he would have gone gallantly through the
discussion and felt the better for his victory.
But he knew that Hugh had spoken for his
sake. He would try not to be such a worry to
them all. He had a bad night, however, and
was, perhaps, not in the best tune the next
morning for trying experiments on himself,
but he would not falter; so, coming down
early, he went into the little back-room,
where they smoked, and kept and cleaned
their guns, and began to look for his own.
He found it in its usual cupboard and took
it out; but the sight, the touch, the very

thought of the sound of it, were more than
he could bear. He just managed to put it
back, and rushed out into the garden. No,
he could never touch it again! But there was
no use in telling anyone that he had such
strange sensations ; and James and his aunt,
only seeing the outside, agreed that he was
as well and cheerful as could be expected.

'My parting advice,' said James, ' is that
everyone should let everybody else alone.'
The shooting was let for a year to Colonel
Dysart without more discussion, and only
Hugh discovered that Arthur shrank from
every trace of it. But, though some of Jem's
words rankled, he was far too much afraid
of seeming to forget his own share in the
matter to offer the support and sympathy
which might have been better than the let-
alone system.

CHAPTER XXXIV.

DIVIDED !

' Again I called, and he could not come.'

DURING the weeks that were so comfortless
and disturbed at Redhurst, Violante's school-
life went on, on the whole, peacefully; but,
still, with various ups and downs of feeling—
fits of longing for Rosa, of loneliness and dis-
couragement ; times when she could not
learn her lessons nor interest herself in the
little trifles that interested her companions.
Yet she never thought of giving in and going
away from Oxley Manor. When she was unhappy she dreaded lest Rosa should discover
it. All the interest of life lay close at hand—

here anything might happen, elsewhere the
scene was closed. Not that Violante gave
herself this reason for her perseverance. No ;
she could not bear to fail a second time ; and
Miss Florence was so kind to her, she was
learning to bear the little rubs of life. So
she mused one soft, fine morning, as she
stood leaning out of the window of the little
upstairs class-room, where she superintended
the girls' practising. As she waited for her
pupils she thought to herself that she was
growing brave and sensible—more like Rosa
—who let nothing interfere with her work.
And then, looking half-expectantly down
the road, she saw a man come by on horse-
back, riding slowly, and looking straight
before him, upright and grave. *She* knew
—*she* saw—*he* did neither ; and, with a sudden impulse, she leant far out of the window
and pulled the little bunch of violets from
her dress and threw them to him, then
darted back behind the curtain. And, as

he started, the violets fell down in the dust; and she saw him laugh and ride on and pass her flowers by. Violante could almost have 'thrown herself out of the window so, in her agony of shame and disappointment. She could not tell whether Hugh knew that she was at Oxley Manor or not—surely he had not intended to repulse her! If he would but smile at her, speak to her!

'If you please, signorina, it's a quarter to ten.'

Violante turned round to encounter a small fat-fingered child in a pinafore, and it counting, 'One, two, three, four,' and mechanically checking wrong notes, as she wondered if he would look up next time that he rode by. When Miss Venning observed shortly afterwards that she thought it would be more convenient if the history classes preceded the practising, which need not then begin till eleven, she little knew what springs she touched. By one accident

and another Violante did not see Hugh again
for a long time; but she did once or twice
encounter Arthur when in company with
Florence, and, therefore, her walks were
haunted by a sense of possibility. She also
occasionally heard Mr. Crichton spoken of at
meal-times as an authority in local matters
under discussion, and gathered that his
opinion was considered important, and that
his judgment was generally supposed to be
severe. It so happened that at this time the
population of Oxley was convulsed with
excitement as to various public improve-
ments then under discussion. There was a
talk of a new branch line of rail between
Fordham and Oxley, and the direction that
this was to take involved local interests of
the most incompatible description. Some
new gas-works were about to be set up by
an enterprising company, and one of the sites
proposed was a field a great deal nearer
Oxley Manor than Miss Venning thought

to be pleasant or profitable for her school. As this field belonged to a certain charity, long ago bequeathed, it was thought that the interests of the poor of Oxley would induce the trustees to dispose of it for a high price to the gas-works.

Miss Venning observed that she was not a person to be put upon without a reason, and that she should represent the matter in the proper quarters.

'If you mean Hugh Crichton,' said Clarissa, 'you may represent it, and he will do exactly what he has already decided upon.'

'Well, my dear, I shall take care that he has the proper information on which to decide; so I shall ask him to call, and show him the field from the windows, so that he can judge for himself.'

So the tones that were associated for Violante with music and flowers, tenderness and love, first fell on her ears to the following effect :

'But you are aware, Miss Venning, that the gas-works must be somewhere? That field is very convenient for them, and I really think it is too far off to cause you any annoyance.'

'Now, Hugh, I'll thank you just to step into the little school-room and look out of window. No, you'll not disturb the girls. Never mind them.'

Violante rose up with her companions as Miss Venning entered. She stood a little behind the others, and could suppose that Hugh did not see her, as he walked up to the window and looked, or pretended to look, out.

'It's a very healthy situation,' he said, vaguely.

'Healthy! And, pray, what consequence can it be to gas-works if they are healthy or not? They would spoil my view; and, really, between them and the railroad, the place won't be worth living in much longer.'

'It doesn't rest with me, you know, Miss Venning. Can you suggest a better situation?'

'I should place them the other side of the town,' said Miss Venning, with decision, ' out towards Blackwood.'

'Yes,' said Hugh, still staring out of the window and hearing nothing.

It may seem a somewhat contemptible state of mind to record; but Hugh was overpowered by a sense of embarrassment, of utter uncertainty as to what to do, as to how to greet her. Why should he evade the previous acquaintance acknowledged by James and Arthur? And yet he felt there was but one way in which he *could* speak to her. As he half turned, and hesitated as he talked confusedly to Miss Venning, the class of girls filed out of the room. Violante passed him. All the short-lived fire of her nature was roused by his hesitation. She gave him no glance of appealing timidity or hopeless love.

She flung up her head and looked at him
with an indignation such as he had never
dreamt of seeing in her soft eyes, and, in
answer to his confused bow, she made the
slightest of curtseys and walked out of the
room.

'You have met Mr. Crichton?' said
Clarissa, who had been with the class.

'Yes, Miss Clarissa, at my father's classes,
but I have no acquaintance with him. It
was Mr. Spencer who met us at Caletto.
Come, Katie—come, Agnes. Your exercises
have too many faults. I shall scold.' And
she sat down and took up her pen, and felt
for the moment as if she could defy every
turn of fortune. Clarissa looked at her, and
went back to where Hugh, confused and
wretched, was talking at random, having
heard Violante's parting shot. She had
turned the tables on him; she was no vision,
no holiday dream, as he had sometimes
called her; but a living woman, first mis-

judged and then neglected. *He* might be right and self-denying, might be giving up his greatest good for the sake of others; but she was wronged, and she had made him feel it.

'I have given it all up!—all—to make some slight atonement for the wrong I have done,' he thought; 'and I must seem a sneak and a scoundrel to myself. How little they know! What a lie life is! If I were a boy I'd run away to sea and have done with it. And I must go this eternal round of committees and business—and—*gas*-works—' with passionate impatience at the momentary matter in hand, as he hurried away, having wildly pledged himself to vote for the locating of the gas-works in the midst of Lord Lidford's park at Blackwood.

He was stung to the very quick by Violante's anger, yet he had made up his mind that all should be at an end between them, and he had too much self-respect to

try 'to make the worse appear the better
reason,' and to offer her any explanation,
since he withheld the one that was her due.
Perhaps, the very renewal of regret that the
sight of her face—more womanly and more
beautiful than when he had left her—caused
him was a sort of support, as it strengthened
the sense of self-sacrifice.   But he was
sufficiently upset and perturbed by what had
passed to forget one or two important
pieces of business, and was forced to accept
Arthur's help in hastily repairing his neglect,
though he had begun the day by resolving
that he would not let much work fall on his
cousin when the soft spring weather made
him look so pale and languid.

With Violante anger was a short-lived
passion, and an hour had not passed before she
longed to recall her scornful words and look,
before she was making a hundred excuses for
her lover. The sight of Hugh in his own place
affected her as it, doubtless, had, however

unconsciously, affected him. She felt miles
farther away from him here in his own town
than among the flowers of Italy. The
pleasant novelty around her was beginning
to lose its effect; she began to grow scared
and stupid, to be again the little helpless
Violante of Civita Bella.

One afternoon—it was a half-holiday—
Miss Florence came sweeping into the school-
room, penetrating it like a fresh sunny
wind, darting into its corners, touching the
sports, employments, humours of all its inhabitants, criticising a drawing, suggesting
a book, adjusting a little quarrel; fresh cur-
rents of air seemed to follow her bright
flaxen head as she whisked about till she
beheld Violante standing by herself in the
window and looking very disconsolate.

'Why, signorina, what's the matter?'

'I am so sorry, Miss Florence.'

'Sorry, what for?'

'La signora is displeased with me.'

'My sister? Is she? Why, what have you been doing?'

Violante blushed, and with much confusion answered that they had been reading English poetry, and something in it made her cry. 'Only a little, Miss Florence,' but the girls laughed and she had burst into tears, and Miss Venning had told her she ought to command her feelings better.

'Well, don't let them get the better of you now,' said Flossy. 'What was this dreadfully touching poem?'

'It was a play called Hamlet, Miss Florence, and he was angry with the girl who loved him.'

'The sentiment was not sufficiently disguised, as our old English teacher used to say,' said Flossy, laughing heartily. 'Did you feel as if you might act Ophelia?'

'Signorina, it seemed too true for acting. It is not like an opera. It might be oneself. But I should not have cried at it.'

'No. School-girls don't like sentiment. But, come, it doesn't signify. My sisters are out. Come into the drawing-room and have some tea with me ; and I want to sing something to you and ask your advice.' Violante followed gladly into the cheerful drawing-room, with its sunny flowery windows, and its look of feminine pleasantness. She sat down in a low easy chair and rested passively. She was tired of her own emotions ; she wanted Rosa. Miss Florence was kind, and bright, and strong, but she did not dare to creep into her arms and lay her head on her shoulder—she did not dare even to cry over her troubles. Excellent discipline, doubtless, but, perhaps, the hardest that could have been devised for so dependent a creature.

'Miss Florence,' she said, after a minute ; 'did Hamlet ever forgive Ophelia?'

'Why, don't you know? She went mad and drowned herself,' said Flossy, cheerfully.

'I wonder how miserable anyone must be before they go mad!'

'Why,' said Florence, as she sat down and began to knit some bright wools together, quite ready for a lively discussion on the characters of the play. 'I suppose no one would who had a well-balanced mind to begin with.'

'I am sure Rosa would not,' said Violante, thoughtfully.

'No, your sister looks like the last person to do anything so silly,' said Flossy, laughing.

'But when there are long years, and friends are cruel, and one has a hard fate, and there is nothing in the world that could happen to set it right——'

The deep, passionate trouble in her voice made Florence look up surprised: she was constantly puzzled by the mixture of ignorance and experience in this girl whose life had been so unlike her own.

'You know, Violante,' she said, 'we are
Christians, and so we must not despair.'

Violante looked perplexed and thoughtful ; yet the words had a meaning for her,
for these weeks had been in one respect a
period of development. She had from the
first taken very kindly to the religious prac-
tices which were observed at Oxley Manor,
and set to work to cure her deficiency in
religious knowledge. Whether because she
thought it was English, or because she wished
to imitate Flossy, or from some blessed instinct leading her to what was for her good,
she showed a love for going to church and
for all sorts of Church teaching which the
Miss Vennings were half-inclined to ascribe
to novelty only. Many of the girls were
under preparation for Confirmation, and she
acquiesced eagerly in the suggestion that she
should join their number. They were care-
fully taught by the Oxley clergy ; and Flossy,

who was an enthusiastic Sunday-school
teacher, had delighted in explaining difficulties and doctrines to the little Italian. How
much Violante comprehended intellectually
may be doubtful, but she began to see better
reasons for trying to do what was distasteful
than the fear of being scolded, began to have
some notion of abstract duties. This she
was carefully taught ; but it was surely no
human words, but the blessing of God on
her innocent humble spirit, that opened her
loving heart to a new and Divine love. There
dawned upon her the thought of a Friend
Who was with her when Rosa was away,
Who loved her when Hugh was cold.
It was but a dim conception, but it had
capabilities of growth. Hymns and texts
were something more than words, and her
endeavours to fulfil these new requirements
had something of the fervour of enthusiasm.
She used to forget the new comfort, let it be
swept away in the tumult of exciting feeling ;

but when the thought came back it was like Rosa's kiss when she was in trouble and disgrace. Flossy's hint recalled it now, and she said, with childish directness:

'Because our Saviour loves us. Ah! I love Him very much!'

There was something in the soft, earnest *naïveté* that made the words touching and sweet even to the English Florence, with whom reverence and reality meant reserve, and who, however she had felt, would have thought such an avowal presumptuous.

'Then, you must try to be good, Violante,' she said, rather repressively.

'Yes,' said Violante, 'and then He will be pleased with me.'

Florence had taught this truth hundreds of times; but she had never heard it thus echoed and claimed; and it came with a new force, as the Bible words are said to do when read in a strange language.

CHAPTER XXXV.

MR. BLANDFORD OF FORDHAM.

'Like some long childish dream
Thy life has run.'

EASTER was now drawing near, but, owing to
the approaching Confirmation and one or
two other reasons connected with the girls'
studies, though some of the pupils went
home, there was no general break-up of the
school; and a week's holiday was to be given
in the beginning of May, when Violante was
to go to London and meet her father, who
was then expected in England. Moreover,
the Miss Vennings, interested in the affection
between the two lonely sisters, invited Rosa
to spend a few days at Easter, and see for

herself what sort of home Violante had found, and to this meeting Violante herself looked forward with a mixture of delight and alarm, as she reflected on the facts hitherto concealed from her sister.

In the meantime Redhurst had filled up all the leisure in Flossy's busy life; and, perhaps, more than all the leisure in her busy soul. She was always welcome there, with her inveterate freshness and brightness, which even the associations of the place could not destroy; she was almost the only visitor whom Arthur really liked to see; and, consequently, the only one to whose coming Hugh did not object. But she was not encouraged to bring Violante there with her, Mrs. Crichton secretly thinking that the young men had talked quite enough about their old acquaintance with her, and Miss Venning being by no means desirous of bringing about a renewal of it. So Hugh only suffered from hearing her progress and her charms de-

scribed by the unconscious Flossy to Arthur,.
while he expressed a hope that 'she had.
forgotten the manager.'

Flossy was too busy a person to be entirely absorbed in one subject; but beneath
all her daily occupations Redhurst was for
ever present in her mind, and—though she
was herself scarcely aware of it—Redhurst
as it affected Arthur Spencer. She never
heard of any incident taking place there
without wondering whether it was pleasant
or not to him ; and, though she did not rival
Hugh in the keenness of his self-conscious
insight into the passing phases of Arthur's-
humour, her sympathy enabled her to draw
much kinder, and, on the whole, truer con-
clusions from them. For Arthur was in an
unsatisfactory state, languid and inconsistent,.
sometimes indolent and careless, and sometimes over-vehement as to his work, in a way
really trying to Hugh's patience; sometimes.
silent and listless, and sometimes apparently

excited by any change, and even ready to
seek it in the companionship of the young
Dysarts and Ribstones. He was so uncertain
as to be sometimes very provoking; but he
did not look well; and Hugh, though secretly
despising what he thought want of self-
control, was outwardly marvellously patient,
when his own secret fretting vexations were
considered. Flossy did Arthur a great deal
of good. She believed in his faith, patience,
and courage, and helped to create the qualities
that she believed in. She liked to coax him
into an argument, to induce him to tease her in
the old fashion, and she was the only person
to whom he ever mentioned Mysie's name,
or to whom he ever talked about himself. All
this was very good for Arthur, who sorely
needed a friend; but, even for the simple
unsentimental Flossy, it was very dangerous
work. How long the peculiar circumstances
of the case might have blinded her eyes to
her danger may be doubtful, as an incident

happened, extremely startling to her in itself,
and which caused her to make a still more
startling discovery. At twenty-one she had
never even been accredited with an admirer,
and had thought far less of young men than
of young maidens ; but, of late, possibilities
had begun to dawn on the minds of her
sisters. A short time before Colonel Dysart
had taken Ashenfold the living of Fordham
had been given to a connection of his, a
Mr. Blandford, who had made some stir in
the clerical world of Oxley by his fine ser-
mons and by the superior manner in which
he organised his new parish. He was about
five-and-thirty and unmarried ; and, through
a whole dinner-party, was observed to discuss
Church matters, practical and theoretical,
with Miss Florence Venning, who dearly
loved good conversation.

'So exactly the sort of man to suit
Flossy!' said Miss Venning, confidentially, to
Clarissa. 'So superior and with such kindred
tastes!'

'It's much too good to be true,' said Clarissa, with one of her quaint little grimaces. 'I shouldn't wonder if he is in favour of the celibacy of the clergy.'

'Oh, my dear, with that nice vicarage! But I'm sure I don't wish to lose Flossy. She is young enough yet.'

Flossy was much flattered at finding that Mr. Blandford adopted some of her suggestions in his Sunday-school, and even went so far as to pity his parish for having no lady to look after it, and to wish that he could prepare the girls for their Confirmation; but, though she met Mr. Blandford tolerably often, she did not regard him in the light of a probable lover, till one morning, as she read her letters at breakfast, Miss Florence's pink cheeks grew redder and redder, and at the first opportunity she pursued her sisters into the drawing-room, and, with a sort of half-dignified fright, communicated the alarming

fact that Mr. Blandford had actually made
her an offer.

'My dear Flossy! Well, it is no surprise
to me,' said Miss Venning.

'I'm sure it's a surprise to me,' said
Flossy, rather ruefully.

'Why, you don't mean to say you never
thought of it?' said Clarissa.

'I did,' said Flossy, 'of course, when
everyone was wondering if he would marry;
but, as he never paid me any attentions, I
decided that—that he would not.'

'Never paid you attention?'

'Why, you don't call talking about Sun-
day-schools and districts attention, do you?'
said Flossy.

'That depends. Did you expect him to
talk about hearts and darts and forget-me-
nots?' laughed Clarissa.

'I thought anyone would do *something*,'
cried Flossy, crimson and nervous, as she
twisted the letter in her hand.

'My dear, don't be so childish,' said Miss
Venning. 'You are startled ; but, depend
upon it, Mr. Blandford's feelings are just as
sincere as if he had talked more about them.
And I'm sure a more excellent person——'

Miss Venning paused, rather overcome by
her feelings ; and Flossy said, gravely :

'I am afraid I *have* been childish. It is
because I think so much of the things that
interest me. But, indeed, I didn't mean to—
to flirt and lead him on.'

'Whatever you meant, my dear,' said
Miss Venning, 'you see the result.'

'What in the world shall I do, Mary?
What shall I say?'

'Why, my darling, if you can care about
him——'

'Oh, dear, no!' interrupted Flossy. 'Of
course, I can't say yes. I never dreamt of
such a thing!'

'Flossy, don't be such a goose!' suddenly
cried Clarissa. 'Do bring your mind down

to the realities of life, and think of something
besides school-girls.'

'If one mayn't talk to an old clergyman
about his parish,' cried Flossy, who was
chiefly concerned in exculpating herself from
the dreadfully unfamiliar notion of having
trifled with the lover's feelings.

'Old! Flossy, you are *too* silly,' said
Clarissa, angrily. But Miss Venning interposed:

'Now give yourself time to recover.
Mr. Blandford should have tried to prepare
your mind for it. Go up to your room and
think it over, and try to understand yourself.'

Miss Venning spoke somewhat as if
Flossy had been a naughty child; but the
girl was glad of the respite, and hurried
away to her own room. There she soon
began to recover herself. A lover in the
flesh is a startling novelty to many maidens
of this latter nineteenth century, and Flossy's
heart had not prepared her so to regard

Mr. Blandford. Her sisters were unmarried, and she had thought it very likely that she should not marry herself. But she had no doubt as to her own feelings, and too much sense to reproach herself after the first flutter was over. It was a simple, honest, womanly answer that she was beginning to write, when a knock interrupted her, and Clarissa came in.

'Flossy,' she said, in an agitated voice, 'Don't—don't be a silly child! You don't know what you are throwing away.'

'Indeed, Clary!' said Flossy, 'I am quite sure that I do not love Mr. Blandford. I am *very* sorry. I misunderstood him, but I am quite clear in my own mind; and if I talked nonsense at first it was just the fluster of the thing.'

'Oh, Flossy, you don't know,' said Clarissa, with tears in her eyes. 'Don't be in a hurry! You think your life will always be like it is now; but you'll get tired of it

—you will, indeed. You'll want something
more. You'll grow into a woman—and—
and you will have missed your chance, and
you'll be sorry.'

'Do you wish me to accept him for the
sake of being married?' said Flossy, in
superb disdain.

'Oh, I cannot tell,' said Clarissa. 'But,
Flossy, I want you to think what you are
making up your mind to. Girls now-a-days
don't have many chances, and, though you're
handsome, you are not so very taking. Don't
you see that it means, perhaps, never to be
married—never to have—— Flossy, think,
think ! '

'Why, Clarissa, anyone would think you
had said no yourself and repented.'

'I? I never said no—nor yes either.'

'You can't suppose I am going to marry
a man I don't love ? '

'No; but there are different ways of
putting things, and if there is no one else——'

'Is it likely?' interrupted Flossy. 'Clarissa, how can I go and marry a man when I don't care as much for him as for hundreds of things—as I care for you and Mary, and the girls——'

'Or Arthur Spencer?' whispered Clarissa, with a sudden mischievous twinkle.

Flossy stood still; a great throb passed through her, and she quivered to her finger-tips.

'Oh, Flossy, Flossy, forgive me,' cried Clarissa, clinging to her. 'Indeed, I didn't know—I didn't mean to——'

'No!' said Flossy, putting her little, slight sister back, and standing up, tall and straight; her blue eyes lightening as they had never lightened before. 'No! I don't care half so much for him as I do for Arthur Spencer— as I did for my dear Mysie. I care exceedingly for Arthur, and Mr. Blandford is only an acquaintance. You said no harm, Clarissa.'

She stood grandly to her colours; but

the sharp-eyed Clarissa saw it all. She ceased her arguments—they had their answer.

'You've got your life-story, anyhow,' she said, ' and you will do as you please. I haven't got any experience to give you the benefit of.'

It is sometimes thought impossible that a woman should give her heart away, wholly without solicitation, utterly without hope of return; and, perhaps, the fire of passion cannot be quite spontaneous. But, whatever Flossy's young, fresh nature understood by love, the absorbing interest, the unselfish devotion, the romantic idealism had gone out to Arthur Spencer, as she thought, for ever. To use an expression prevalent among the gentle, self-restrained heroines of an earlier day, ' she had allowed her affections to become engaged,' and she faced the fact with all her natural sense and honesty. He was the one man in the world for her, and she would have——

Poor Flossy burst into tears of shame

and fright as she thought that there was
nothing she would not have done for his
sake. But as she was not ' disappointed,'
as she had never for a moment connected
any personal hopes or fears with him, she
could bear to think that this feeling must be
carried about with her, hopeless of result;
without being utterly wretched, or fancying
that she could never care for life again. And
as she was proud and brave, and was his
true friend before all things, she could resolve
to make no perceptible change in her behaviour, but to be as kind to him as ever, while
no single soul should guess *how* kindly she
felt. The idea had its attraction. Flossy's
young eyes were half-blinded by the sunrise
still; her loves and her sorrows had still some
of the fascination of romance, were still fresh
from the stately dreamland of hero-worship
and self-sacrifice. And so, fearless, she
turned her back on cloudland, and came
out ' into the light of common day,' which

would soon show the stones in her path
plainly enough. But as she was sensible and
practical too, and not inexperienced—if experience can ever be other than personal—she
was aware also that it was an unlucky thing
that had come to her, and one to solemnise,
if not sadden, her life ; and she was seized
with a fit of self-distrust. ' I feel as if my
case was just the one exception to all rules;
but I never heard any girl talk nonsense who
didn't think *that*,' she said, bitterly, to herself. ' Well, any way, someone has liked
me,' and with that she burst into a great
flood of tears ; and, though she was far too
single-minded to waver in her determination,
the result of her discovery that she had given
her heart to another was that poor Mr.
Blandford received a much softer and more
tenderly-expressed refusal than he would
have got before, and that she thought of him
with a much greater amount of gratitude.
However, between tears and excitement, she

had worried herself into a bad headache, and
was quite unable to go down to her teaching
—a circumstance nearly as unusual as the
event which had caused it, and which cost
her another half-hour's argument before she
could convince Miss Venning that she did
not regret her decision, and could induce her
anxious sister to leave her in peace. She had
been lying on her bed, half-asleep, for some
time, when there was a little tap, and Violante
came in with a cup of coffee in her hand.

'Miss Clarissa said I might bring you
this. Are you better, signorina mia ?'

'Oh, yes,' said Flossy, sitting up. 'My
headache is gone, I think. Thank you,
Violante; this is very good. Oh, dear!
Whatever became of the Italian ?'

'I did it, Miss Florence, all myself; and
Miss Clarissa sat in the room,' said Violante,
in accents of pride.

'Why, Violante, how clever you are
getting!'

'Ah, Miss Florence, I would do anything to help you a little bit!' said Violante, kissing her hand. 'The house is sad when you are ill.'

Flossy was in a soft mood, and thought that she might yield to the girl's caressing sweetness, without the possibility of a suspicion that she was fretting for Mr. Fordham or for anyone else. She little thought that Violante—who, it is to be feared, considered being in love as the normal condition of young maidens, and who had heard Florence talk a great deal about Arthur—was only deterred from guessing the true state of the case by her conviction that such a being as Miss Florence could only find her equal in 'Signor Hugo.' To be sure, when, in a fit of holiday-gossip, some glib-tongued girl had made this suggestion, Edith Robertson had silenced her with a sharp 'Oh, dear, no; not likely at all! Mr. Crichton will marry into a county family,' which remark had seemed

to show innumerable vistas between *herself*
and Hugh ; still, *could* Flossy know him and
be insensible? Flossy little guessed these
thoughts, as Violante caressed her and helped
her to twist up her long bright hair—the
flossy flaxen—which the little Italian girl
thought the most beautiful colour in the
world; and Florence was comforted, she
hardly knew how, and went once more about
her business, perhaps a little graver, a little
less ready for unnecessary interests; but
giving Miss Venning no reason to suppose
that she regretted Mr. Blandford. When she
looked back on her interview with Clarissa
it struck her that sister's manner had been
singular; and one day she said to Miss Venning : ' Mary, did Clarissa ever have any
lovers ? '

' Never, my dear, that I know of. I
wish she had. She doesn't like girls, and
would be happier married.'

' Nor ever cared for anyone ? '

'Not that I know of,' answered Miss Venning, placidly, as she folded the letter that she had been writing to an anxious mother to relate her daughter's progress and well-being. Flossy reflected; but her own memory did not come to her aid; for, indeed, there was nothing to remember, and Clarissa subsided into her usual lazy, satirical, yet not uncheerful, demeanour; sharp-eyed and sharp-tongued; always the provider of the family jokes and the arranger of the little family comforts, the easy-chairs and cups of tea and unexpected fires, of which she always showed such a strong appreciation. Yet it occurred to Flossy for the first time to wonder what was Clarissa's main-spring. Certainly not her work, which she hated; nor any art or occupation, for she had none of any great consequence; and not her sisters, for she did not often excite herself about their concerns. It seemed an objectless life; could Clarissa have mended it? Flossy, young and enthusiastic, was much inclined to answer that she could ; and yet it was very difficult to imagine Clarissa taking up any of the lines that seemed so alien to her. She could no more acquire Flossy's strong impulses and inborn tastes than she could alter the outlines of her lot ; no more give herself a love than a lover.

CHAPTER XXXVI.

AMONG THE PRIMROSES.

'Who on faint primrose-beds were wont to lie.'

'ROSA—ROSA, carissima mia! To see you —to have you again! I have wanted you every day!'

'My darling child, I don't know when I have not wanted *you!* Tell me all—everything. Are you well—are you happy? I think you look so.'

'We have tried to make her so,' said Flossy, as Rosa withdrew from Violante's clinging embrace to look into her face and read its story. 'Now, Violante, make your sister comfortable, and all the rest of us are going to walk.'

Left thus alone, Violante put Rosa into a chair and knelt at her feet, looking up in her face. Rosa was looking remarkably well and handsome; she was nicely dressed, and had an air of prosperity.

'And so they are very kind to you?' she said.

'They are as kind as angels,' said Violante, 'and there is no one like Miss Florence except you.'

Rosa laughed, and Violante went on, rather hurriedly:

'And our cousins,—how are they? And your pupils—are they stupid? How far have they got in Italian?'

'Not very far,' said Rosa; 'and that's the first question you ever asked me about a pupil in your life.'

'But I teach a great deal of the Italian.

VOL. III.   H

Miss Florence showed me how. And father —will he come soon?'

'Yes. I'm afraid, Violante, he has not found much to do in Florence. I shall be glad when he comes to London, because I think he is likely to get engagements.'

'Does he know anyone in London?' asked Violante.

'Well—there is a gentleman who comes a good deal to Uncle Grey's,' said Rosa, colouring a little. 'He is not exactly a professional musician; but he loves music better than anything, and he has composed some things—they're very good, I think. He said he would ensure some engagements for father. So we shall get some nice little lodgings near the Greys. I know some that would do for us, and when you come, darling—it will be home again.'

'And father is coming ——?'

'The first week in May.'

'Yes, and our holidays are to be on the

7th. You know we should have gone home now, but for the Confirmation ; and, besides, Miss Venning's brother, who is a clergyman, is coming to examine the school on the 5th of May in arithmetic and those hard lessons ; so the classes preparing for him have not broken up.'

'How funny it sounds to hear you talk about lessons and arithmetic! Can *you* do your sums, my child?'

'Not very well,' replied Violante, modestly ; ' they are very often wrong, Rosina. But I have learnt many things.'

She turned and slipped down by Rosa's side, playing with her fingers ; but keeping her own face averted.

'Things are very strange, Rosa mia. I never expected to see Signor Arthur here.'

'Signor Arthur. Mr. Spencer? *Here.* Where?' exclaimed Rosa, greatly surprised.

'Yes,' said Violante, trying to control her trembling, ' he—that is, *they*, live

here at Redhurst. They are Miss Venning's
friends.'

'*They*—you don't mean Mr. Crichton!
Oh, Violante, if I had known this——' then,
as there was a pause, 'Have you seen
him?'

'Oh, yes. But he never spoke, nor I to
him. Do not fear, Rosa. He is a great
gentleman, and he knows well *here* that I
am only a poor little girl; and no one
knows anything.'

'Oh, my darling, you should not have
stayed here an hour!'

'Then you would be more foolish than
I,' cried Violante; 'more foolish a great deal,
Rosa. You see I am well and happy. And
is not a girls' school like a convent? I never
see any of them but Signor Arthur, and he
is always kind. His *promessa sposa* was here
at school, you know, Rosa. She was Miss
Florence's dear friend.'

'I could not have believed that you

would have concealed such a thing from me!' said Rosa, reproachfully.

'It was because I knew you would expect me to be unhappy. I wanted you to see me and to know that I can bear it,' said Violante, with excitement. 'Rosa, I would not deceive you—it is all over—all over! But I knew you would hear their names.'

'Mr. Spencer Crichton, then, is an acquaintance of Miss Venning's?' said Rosa, still in a tone of perturbation.

'Yes; and, besides, he has to do with everything—the railways and the gas——'

'The what?'

'Why, they were going to build some ugly gas-works in the field, and he was the only person who could prevent it. That was why he came here. But it is Signor Arthur who is their friend.'

'Ah, has he got over his trouble?'

'No,' said Violante, with an air of interest and knowledge rather surprising to Rosa.

'Oh, no, he looks much more sad and ill than he did in Italy. I think he will never forget Mysie. But they will be coming in, and I was to show you your room. There,' as Rosa followed her, 'that is the school-room, and I must go there presently and see that the little girls get ready for tea.'

Rosa felt utterly bewildered. It is always startling to find one's nearest and dearest possessed with a flood of new ideas and interests, acquired apart from ourselves, and this is specially the case with a girl's first experience of independent life. Violante's very accent and idiom had attained a more English turn, and there was an air of life and capability about her entirely new. She had opinions and ideas, and evidently was proud of her various occupations and anxious to show them off. How much of this was owing to her more vigorous health—the English air evidently being very favourable to her—how much to the mental awakening

which some congenial experience often gives
to girls sooner or later, and how much to
the undercurrent of excitement that Hugh
Crichton's neighbourhood caused, Rosa could
not tell. Certainly she was glad to see her
little sister so bright and well; but she could
not get over the idea of Violante's secresy,
and forgot, perhaps, how hardly while pitying
her sister she had judged Hugh in her hearing. Moreover, Rosa's attention was not so
entirely devoted to Violante's affairs as had
been the case last year. Possibilities were
arising in her own life; but they were still
too vague for her to wish to make a confi-
dante of her young sister. There seemed to
be what the Miss Greys called 'a chance for
Rosa;' and Rosa, it was thought, was not
altogether averse to avail herself of it. She
was very agreeable, and her foreign experi-
ences and shrewd cleverness gave her an
originality refreshing in a London young
lady. She liked society; and, besides, she

liked attention, in a sensible moderate sort
of way ; at any rate, she liked the attentions
of the musical Mr. Fairfax. He was not a
very young man, and not at all handsome ;
but he had enough enthusiasm of character
to appeal to Rosa's sympathies, and enough
of unconventionality to think her history and
connections attractive rather than the reverse.
He held a situation in the British Museum,
and had some private means ; so that he had
been able to indulge his musical taste without
being dependent on it for support. Nothing
very definite had passed, but he was gradually giving Rosa to understand that he
meant something serious ; and she had wel-
comed this short absence as an opportunity
for making up her own mind and testing her
own feelings.

She made a very good impression on
Miss Venning, and became friendly with
Flossy, though secretly she thought her
rather high-flying, and considered her ob-

jects of interest inadequate to the enthusiasm expended on them. She found that Violante, allowance being made for her imperfect education, was considered to have fair capabilities; and, with the help of her music and Italian, to be likely to be able to earn her living, under favourable circumstances. ('If I had a home for her to fall back upon,' was Rosa's mental comment;) while she was much liked by teachers and companions. Rosa was constantly amused and surprised at seeing her busy and important; but, perhaps, she liked the moments best when Violante nestled down by her side, happy once more in her caressing presence. Rosa had arrived on Easter Monday, and was to stay till Saturday. The Confirmation would take place on the Friday, and on the Wednesday afternoon the whole party went into the woods to gather primroses, to renew the Easter decoration of Oxley parish church. The best primroses grew near Fordham; but, as nothing would have tempted Miss Florence's steps in that direction, she ordained that they should walk towards Oxley—'it was a prettier view to show Miss Mattei.'

All along the opposite banks of the canal, between Fordham, Redhurst, and Oxley—and, indeed, out beyond Blackwood, on the other side of the town—were, at intervals, great oak copses, skirting the heath behind. Ashenfold was in the midst of them; they touched at one end the famous Fordham beeches, and at the other were lost in Lord Lidford's park at Blackwood. The London road crossed the canal by a bridge at Oxley, where the woods were interspersed with villas, and a path, rough and dirty in winter, but charming in summer, led right through them to Redhurst and Fordham. A sort of hand-bridge led back to the Redhurst Road, opposite Ashenfold; further on there were only Redhurst and Fordham locks.

A considerable tract of copse had been

felled the year before; and this spring the
place of the underwood was supplied by the
young sprouting oak-shoots and by myriads
of primroses and anemones, ivy, lichen and
moss, and all the beauties of woodlands in
the spring. It was a lovely day, warm and
sunny, with a sky the colour of the speed-
wells that were still hiding in the hedges.
Birds sang and twittered; butterflies, like flying primroses, hovered about in pairs.

'There is nothing like a wood in spring,'
said Florence; 'and out there, Miss Mattei,
the furze is getting golden, and even that
ploughed field has a deep, rich colour under
this wonderful sky.'

'Yes, abroad we don't believe in English
spring, but a day like this——'

'Vindicates the spring of the poets—and
makes up for rain and east winds, doesn't it?'

The girls scattered over the wood in
search of their primroses, Violante among
them; while Rosa sat down on a log and

talked to Miss Venning. The chatter and
laughter of the girls sounded through the
wood; and Flossy, in her great straw hat, with
her hands full of primroses, came back towards them over the rough broken ground,
tall, lithe, and blooming, like an incarnation
of this fresh woody spring. Suddenly she
paused, and exclaimed, as Hugh and Arthur,
in rather unwonted companionship, came up
the narrow path towards her.

'What? A great primrose-picking?' said
Arthur.

'Yes, did you come to enjoy the woods?'
she said.

'I wanted to go to Ashenfold,' said Hugh,
'so we came back this way. We are rather
idle this week.'

As he spoke, Hugh became aware of
Rosa's presence, by hearing Arthur greet
her; and, after a momentary hesitation on
both sides, they bowed, and he asked after
Signor Mattei.

'My father is very well, thank you,' said
Rosa, without an unnecessary word. Hugh
stood like a shy boy in his first quadrille, trying
to think of something that would do to say.
Arthur had strolled away towards the prim-
rose-pickers, and he decided that it would
look too marked to walk on without him.
At last he said: 'Oh! Miss Venning, about that
gas. I believe I shall get it arranged as you wish.'

'I always knew, Hugh, that no sensible
person could see it in any other light,' said
Miss Venning.

'I don't think gas is injurious to human
life,' said Hugh, looking round the wood.
Rosa almost pitied him, he seemed so ill at
ease. 'The component parts——'

'Now, I am said to be fond of discussions,' said Flossy; 'but, really, to talk chemi-
cally in this lovely wood is a shame.'

'Let us come, then, and look at the view
and find Arthur,' said Hugh, relieved; 'I
ought to be going.'

Rosa would fain have followed, but Miss Venning, with a ' You see, my dear,' entered on the subject of the gas-works, and the other two walked farther into the wood.

There were days when Hugh was sure that he ought not to marry Violante, there were many days when he thought that he did not wish to marry her; but now and then came a day when he dreamed of a future that might come when time should have softened the present troubles, and this day was one of them. He would *not* throw away this chance—at least, he would see her and hear her speak again. Suddenly the sound of her sweet unmistakable voice fell on his ear. They were coming over a piece of rising ground, and down below them sat Arthur and Violante on a fallen tree. She was tying the primroses into little bunches. The occupation and her light spring dress brought another sunny afternoon and other brighter-tinted flowers to Hugh's mind.

He could only see the top of Arthur's hat ;
but her face was visible, raised in profile,
tender and smiling, in the radiant sun. She
was evidently answering a remark.

'Ah, then, do *you* " say die," so often ? '

' Very often, I am afraid.'

' But I keep the olive-leaves, signor, and
I look at them sometimes.'

' Ah, yes, I remember, I believe I have
mine here still,' and Arthur took out his
pocket-book, and after a moment's search
showed the little spray of leaves.

Neither Hugh nor Florence were so con-
ventionally-minded as exactly to misinterpret
the facts of what they had seen ; and, besides,
Arthur's voice and manner were essentially
unloverlike ; but it seemed to Hugh as if
those sweet looks and smiles were for all
alike, awakened by his cousin as well as by
himself. *Something* there was between
them, and what might there not come of it
by and by ? while to Flossy the first sharp

pang of uncontrollable jealousy was not un-
naturally aggravated by Violante's look of
utter confusion and perplexity, as a turn of
her head revealed their presence and they
stepped down the bank beside her.   She
had not known that Hugh was with Arthur.

'You are still fond of flowers, Mademoiselle Mattei?' said Hugh, dryly.

She looked at him.

'These flowers are different,' she said.
Perhaps she hardly knew what she meant.

'Fresher and newer,' said Hugh.   Hugh
was the worst of hypocrites, and Arthur
had never seen him look quite as he looked
now.   Impossible, incredible!

'Flossy,' he began, 'let us come——'
when a sudden outbreak of voices and
laughter near them made them all turn.
Two of the Dysart girls had been of the
party and had previously coaxed their
mother to surprise Miss Venning with a
supply of cake and new milk to be eaten in

the wood, as an impromptu pic-nic, and Mrs. Dysart had now made her appearance, followed by two of her little boys carrying the provisions.

Miss Venning did not emulate the schoolmistress who desired her charges to turn their faces to the hedge when a man passed by; still, she was conscious that Mrs. Dysart might think the situation unusual; while, as for Hugh, he looked so indignant, so ashamed, and so uncomfortable that Rosa could hardly help laughing, and Arthur's face of amusement was a study. But Mrs. Dysart was a lady who took things easily, even the presence of two of her elder sons, who declared that they had followed as the milk was too heavy for their little brothers.

'What quantities of primroses you have got!' she said.

'You see, Hugh picked so many!' said Arthur. He could not resist the little joke,

any more than he could help the bright
courtesy that made him enter into the
spirit of the thing, and pour out the milk
and hand the cake.

'Drink, signorina!' he said, gaily, as he
gave a cup to Violante.

And yet, when the thought came over
him of what such a merry-making would
have been to him last year, perhaps Hugh,
angry and full of miserable misunderstanding
as he was, need hardly have envied his
cousin's smile. For Violante stood, living
and beautiful, before him; and though he
shut his eyes to the sun-rays of possibility,
he felt their warmth.

It was all over in ten minutes. Miss
Venning summoned her flock; Hugh asked
if Colonel Dysart was at home, and, with
Arthur, followed the milk-jugs back to
Ashenfold. Flossy, feeling miserable, cross,
ready to cry, and utterly unheroic, thought
she should hate the sight of primroses for

ever ; and Violante—flushed, excited, knowing that, whatever Hugh's tone indicated, it was *not* indifference—thought the fair, tender blossoms had just a little of the sweetness that had clung to the white bouquet, one precious trophy of her stage-life.

PART VI.

AT THE YEAR'S END.

'This, only this; through sorrow cometh learning,
  Through suffering, greater growth.
In patience, therefore, wait the golden morning
  That draweth near us both.'

CHAPTER XXXVII.

ANOTHER CHANCE.

'Only the sound of a voice,
   Tender and sweet and low—
That made my heart rejoice
   A year ago!'

JAMES CRICHTON was spending a few days
at home, with a view to the proposed oratorio at H——, which was to take place the
week after Easter. He was, however, obliged
to go up to town on most days, and was
rather fond of calling in at the Bank on his
way from the station and walking or driving
back with his brother and Arthur. Perhaps,
this practice had partly induced Hugh's visit
to Ashenfold on the day of the primrose
picnic. For Hugh was not fond of walking

down Oxley High-street with Jem. It was all
very well, he thought, to know every man,
woman, and child in Redhurst, and even to
be on civil terms with the inhabitants of
Oxley ; but Jem carried things too far.

When they passed the greengrocer's—
'Well, Mr. Coleman, how d'ye do? How's
your little girl? Gone to boarding-school?—
hope she'll get on with her French. Why,
Hugh, there's Kitty Morris—how dark her
hair's grown! She's not as pretty as she used
to be.'

'I never saw her before, to my knowledge,' Hugh would probably reply.

'Never saw Kitty—oh, she belongs to
that little print-shop. She's always standing
at the door. I declare, there's old Tomkins !
I must just cross over and speak to him.'

A delay of two or three minutes listening
to old Tomkins ; and then, still worse, an
elaborate bow to two Miss Harrisons—and,
though Hugh knew that neither the popu-

larity nor the familiarity of the 'Oh, Mr. Crichton, '*ow* pleased ma *will* be to see you!' could be intended for him, he would grow desperate, and march on, while Jem would finish up by saying :

'Ah, when you want to represent the borough send me to canvass—that's all!'

Jem had not been at home long before he proposed that Arthur should come back to London with him for the sake of a little change and variety. It was evident, he said, that a change was wanted, and the proposal was eagerly taken up by his mother, who pressed it upon Arthur in a way that hardly left him a choice.

'You see, my dear boy, you don't look well, and are sadly out of spirits,' she said, in her outspoken way; 'and this will be the very thing to do you good.'

'Jem is very kind; but it would not do me any good,' said Arthur.

'Oh, yes, my dear, it will. Change is

always good for people, and you haven't been
much in London.   You know we must all
make efforts.'

'There is nothing the matter with me,'
said Arthur, escaping from the room; while
his aunt went on : 'Poor boy, it's time he
should be a little cheerful, and he is not half
so bright as he was at first.'

'No; that's just what I say,' returned
Jem; 'everything here reminds him of her,
and London will be all fresh.'

Even Flossy Venning was moved to give
the same counsel, which she did with rather
suspicious eagerness, half-afraid to seem unwilling to part with him.   Arthur had no
counter-arguments to urge but his own unwillingness, and this seemed only to prove
the necessity of the measure; but he did not
yield readily, though he half-believed they
were right, and had not the energy to put
an end to the discussion by a more emphatic

refusal. Hugh would not interfere, save by the brief remark :

' Yes, things are wrong ; but it will take more than that to set them right; but at last he said :

' You do not wish to go, Arthur ? '

' Oh, no,' said Arthur, in a sort of matter-of-course tone.

' Is there anything you would like better to do ? ' said Hugh, with the elaborate gentleness with which he often addressed his cousin.

' Oh, no,' said Arthur again. ' I am sorry to make such a bad business of it. Perhaps, I ought to get away somewhere, and not make you all miserable.'

' It is not that,' said Hugh ; ' but Jem is always cheerful ; you and he have tastes in common, and sometimes you do seem brighter for a little amusement.'

' That's only because I'm such a fool, Hugh, you are so wonderfully good to me.

Don't you think I know how I put you out?
I take up with things—sometimes I forget
how I've changed—then I get deadly sick of
it all and tired out. Or else a word—a
look! Oh, I know well enough what I ought
to do; but it's making bricks without straw—
I've no pluck left.'

Perhaps because he *had*, with whatever
shortcomings, tried very hard to be 'good'
to Arthur, perhaps because the confidence
was made to himself, Hugh was able to conceal the personal pain which these passionate
words caused him; and it was with real
tenderness that he answered :

'I think you have shown no want of
pluck ; but when you first talked of coming
back I was afraid you would not be able to
bear it ; this place is full of sword-pricks
for you. Aren't you straining your nerves
too far by staying here?'

Arthur did not answer, and Hugh, watching him as he stood leaning against the

shutter and staring fixedly out into the sunshine, said, with more hesitation :

'Or is it that the want of an aim, of an
object is worse than anything else, and that
you feel less at sea when you are obliged to
do something ? '

'Yes,' said Arthur, quickly. 'Yes. Ah,
you understand! I *want* something to
hold by.'

'But then,' said Hugh, 'you mustn't be
too hard on yourself. You look ill, and
sometimes you feel so ; you don't sleep, and
then you are not fit for these efforts.'

'You seem to know all about me,' said
Arthur; but not as if the comprehension
hurt him.

'Yes, I believe I do,' said Hugh, looking
away from him ; but with a curious sense of
a fresh spring in his heart. Was all that
bitter involuntary watching, that keen,
morbid analysis of Arthur's feelings, which
had cost him so much pain, to bear fruit at

last? Had the sympathetic suffering which
he had looked on as expiation been no fruit-
less penance, but a training that might enable
him to make some poor amends? Was it
possible that he, who had caused and shared
the sorrow, could be the one to comfort and
help?

'I think I do understand,' he said. 'It
will be best for you to stay here quietly, and
join when you can in what goes on, or pass it
by without any comment being made. Only,
you must promise to tell me if you feel that
it is getting too much for you—that is, if you
will,' he added, with a little return to his
self-distrust.

'Oh, yes, I'll tell you, if you don't find
out,' said Arthur, with some of his natural
liveliness; then added, earnestly and affec-
tionately : 'You have done me a great deal
of good.'

Hugh had never felt so nearly happy
since he had come back to England as at

those words. If Arthur could feel so he should never want for comfort again. The first effort at really helping him for his own sake had broken through his self-conscious shrinking; and Hugh felt that, with so ready a response, he could comfort Arthur and find his own consolation in doing it.

There was no doubt of the response. Arthur never theorized about what he could or could not do and feel, and he turned instantly to Hugh's offered comprehension and sympathy. Indeed, he was so easily cheered for the moment, and almost always so bright in manner, that it was difficult to believe how completely he had been thrown off his balance, and how much the strain was telling upon him. It was by his irre- solution and changeableness and excitable vehemence, ending in utter indifference, rather than by absolute low spirits that his grief told. Sometimes he could not decide on the merest trifle, such as a walk *versus* a

ride; and, again, he would involve himself in
some undertaking, just because he was asked
to do so, and then a voice, a look, the name
of a place or a person—anything that jarred
his nerves with a sudden recollection—would
make the act impossible to him. In the
same way, though he rarely had even a
headache to complain of, he was often utterly
unequal to an exertion which another day
would be easy to him.

It was just the state for which change of
scene seemed most desirable; but to which
by itself it would do little good; and it
was well, indeed, for Arthur that fate, or his
own judgment, had placed him where all
this irresolution and want of ballast was
likely to result in nothing worse than idle-
ness and uselessness. Had he been thrown
in the way of temptation at this critical
period neither his own principles nor the
memory of Mysie might have supplied an
adequate resisting force, while he would pro-

bably have broken down under solitude altogether.

That conversation was like the lifting of a veil. Hugh had always known where Arthur's shoe pinched him ; he only needed to act on his knowledge to be the very help that was wanted, and he had not won Arthur's glance of thanks and relief twice before he began to look for it as his own greatest pleasure. Like many severe people when once softened, he was almost over-tender, and could not bear to see his cousin struggle with himself. He would not, therefore, allow the expedition to H—— to be urged upon him ; so Jem, Mrs. Crichton, Frederica, and Flossy set off on the day appointed.

Hugh found time, in spite of this new interest, to display what the Vicar of Oxley called ' a very proper feeling on the part of one of the chief laymen of the parish,' by attending the Confirmation. He had meditated much on the scene of the olive leaves ;

but, in the new light thrown on Arthur's
mind, it had lost much of its sting. Not so
with Flossy. She had never dreamt that
her unselfish love could be marred by such
foolish, miserable jealousy. Did silent devotion mean that she was to be wretched whenever he spoke to another woman? Her
thoughts wandered, her mind was disturbed,
she wondered as to Violante's past history, it
was an effort to think of the scene before her.

Hugh watched Violante from a distance,
and perceived that she was not aware of his
presence. The impressionable Italian nature
was lifted into enthusiasm by the first
religious ceremony in which she had ever
taken part. Her eyes were bright and
tearful, her cheeks flushed. This epoch in
her life did not present itself to her as a
moral crisis, as a new resolve to fulfil difficult duties, a strain after a recollectedness
and gravity respected but hardly attained
to. It came to her as a new happiness, a

new love and a new sense of protection. She was not conscious that she felt differently from her companions; and Flossy watched this beautiful fervour with a sort of awe, even while she half-distrusted it as a lasting motive of action.

Before they left the church a hymn was sung and as Violante's heart swelled with the words and the music, unconsciously she raised her voice too, and its long silent notes smote on her ear, clear and full, as when she had sung last in the opera-house of Civita Bella. She dropped down on her knees and hid her face. Had it come back to her—this invaluable gift, this terrible, beautiful possession? Was her new ease of living to slip away from her, and must she return to the 'pains austere' of the talent which belonged to her and to no other? She had heard a great deal lately about her duty, and for her 'her duty' had always meant singing in public. And her father

was coming; and he had not been successful.   But no one had heard her—no one
would know!   Hitherto she had but help-
lessly yielded to the will of others—*this* was
the first moral struggle she had ever known.
She saw and heard no more of what was
passing till they reached home, when she
escaped from the others and ran away by
herself down to the farther end of the
garden.   She stood still in the shrubbery
under its budding green, and listened.
All was silent, but the twitter of the birds;
and softly, timidly, she began again to sing
the hymn that she had just heard:

'Come, Holy Ghost, our souls inspire!'

and as she went on the notes rose fuller and
clearer, and she could not but rejoice in their
sweetness.   Then she paused, and, with a
sense of desperation, began to sing the
melody so fraught with memories of every
sort, the never-to-be-forgotten 'Batti, batti.'

And, as she sang, Rosa came down the

garden path, and beheld her standing
under the trees, in her white confirmation
dress, and singing the passionate operatic
love-song with a curious look of resolution
on her face. She broke off suddenly, and
threw herself into her sister's arms : 'Rosa,
Rosa! I will be good. I meant to tell
you. My voice, my voice! Oh, father,
father !'

The voice was choked in an agony of
sobs and tears, and Rosa, hardly less agitated, held her in her arms and tried to
soothe her.

As soon as she could speak she sobbed
out : 'It has come back, and—and I will
sing for father—but, oh! I thought I should
stay here always and teach the little ones.'

'Indeed, my darling, you shall not come
away from here yet.'

'No, and I could not act.'

'No, that you never shall; but, darling,
to hear your voice again !'

There was a little pause; then Violante said:

'I may stay here and learn things a little longer—and afterwards I will sing at concerts—if—if—— '

She faced her probable future; but there was still an '*if*' in her life.

CHAPTER XXXVIII.

JEM'S IDEAL.

'Faultily faultless—icily regular—splendidly null.'

THE weather favoured the choir festival
at H—— and the production of spring
dresses for the occasion. James cast critical
eyes on his mother's bonnet and on Frederica's
hat; and anxiously consulted Arthur as to
whether he liked a flower in the button-hole
of a morning.

'Oh, yes, when you want to look festive,'
said Arthur, without paying much attention
till he was roused from the perusal of the
'Times' by a crash in the conservatory; and
on hastening to the rescue perceived Jem,

contemplating the ruins of his mother's best
azalea, which he had knocked over in trying
to reach a bit of fern beyond it. Three
dainty little bouquets were already lying in
a row.

'Well, Jem, you have done it now!'

'Oh, confound the thing, yes—and it's
time to be off. Isn't the carriage there?'

'Not yet. Are you going to wear three
bouquets?'

'No,' said Jem, looking foolish, 'I was
only choosing the best. I think I'll go
without.'

'You couldn't improve on that rosebud,
and it might come in handy,' said Arthur,
gravely.

'Well,' snatching it up. 'Just pick up
that pot. I hear the carriage.'

'Pick up the pot!' ejaculated Arthur,
as Jem rushed away, 'when it's in fifty
pieces! I shall retire before I'm supposed
to have thrown it down. I say, Hugh,' as

he came back to the house, 'who's the attraction at H—— ? Jem is evidently on tenter-hooks.'

It was this easy laughter and readiness to joke on what would have seemed to him a tender subject that had always puzzled Hugh in Arthur; but now he was glad to see him amused on any terms, as he answered, gravely:

'I daresay there are several; but I haven't heard him mention anyone in particular.'

'Perhaps he wanted a bouquet apiece and I've spoiled sport! What a pity!'

James recovered his equanimity as they drove away, and was very smiling and chatty by the time they picked up Flossy, fresh and spring-like, and prepared to enjoy herself, though she had hoped that the party might have been differently constituted. They had about twenty miles to go by train, and James made himself very agreeable to her,

mentally thinking her less overpowering
than usual. He asked after Violante and
listened with much interest to Flossy's account of the return of her voice, and her
subsequent resolution.

'But her sister says she must stay with
us till next year, that she may grow quite
strong and finish her education. She is
going to London in May.'

'Indeed! Perhaps I shall see her there.'

'Is Arthur going with you?' asked
Flossy, who had been meditating on this
simple question ever since she joined them.

'No. Poor boy, he couldn't make up
his mind to it. I should have had to leave
him alone a good deal, and he doesn't seem
up to gaieties.'

'Oh, no!'

'No—he laughed in an odd sort of way
—and said : that I'd better not help him to
cast off from his moorings ; but I'm sure being
at home doesn't answer. He has a bright

way with him; but I see more and more
how he is altered. His eyes have a sort of
wretched look, instead of their old jolly one—
don't you know what I mean?'

'Yes; as if he wanted something.'

'Exactly. I think he'll have to make a
change. I wish he could go abroad and
begin a new life altogether—in India, or
somewhere.'

'Would that be best?' said Florence,
slowly.

'I think so. But there's one thing—Hugh
seems to understand him now, and he has
got excellent judgment when he likes to use
it.'

Poor Flossy! That conversation did not
raise her spirits, or prepare her to enjoy her
day. There was a dreadful probability in
James's suggestion, and she mused over it
while he was talking to his mother and urging her to drive at once to the Archdeacon's.

' My dear, we have our tickets—we shall see them afterwards.'

'But, they have ways and means of getting in, you know; and you would avoid the crowd.'

Mrs. Crichton yielded after a little demur, and they drove to Archdeacon Hayward's, where they were politely received and offered an entrance with the Cathedral ladies, Mrs. Hayward being glad to be civil to Mrs. Spencer Crichton. The girls were introduced to three or four fair, tall young ladies, much alike in dress and demeanour, with aquiline features and graceful figures, and a very proper amount of conversation. Jem sat profoundly silent, with his hat in his hand and his rosebud in his coat, till one of the Miss Haywards, *not* Helen, said:

'You are fond of music, I believe, Mr. Crichton?'

'Oh, devotedly!' said Jem, smiling.

'And there is nothing like Handel?'

'Very fine!' said James.

'Why, Jem, I thought you despised him?' said Freddie, abruptly. 'I thought he wasn't a new light.'

'Is that one of your heresies, Mr. Crichton?' said another Miss Hayward, from behind; and Jem turned round, with startling rapidity, and asked who had been setting him down as a heretic?

As the oratorio took place in the Cathedral the conversation was limited, but Mrs. Crichton was gratified by observing that Jem sat peacefully with his own party, discovered no odd acquaintances, and afterwards returned with them to the Archdeacon's, where there was a large party to luncheon.

Miss Helen Hayward was polite to Mrs. Crichton, who remarked to Frederica how nice it was to see girls attentive to their guests, and not forgetful, or taken up with their own affairs.

'Yes, auntie; but she always talks in the

same tone of voice,' said Freddie, suspecting a didactic motive.

Flossy had a dull neighbour at lunch, and leisure to look about her, and she felt inclined to pity Jem, who sat opposite by the third Miss Hayward, whose mild restrained smiles and obvious, if intelligent, remarks did not strike her as very interesting. Presently, however, she perceived that James had more and more to say on his side; that he made Miss Helen laugh and blush, and look at her plate, and then across the table to see if her sisters were noticing her. This amused Flossy, but she was surprised to observe that Jem looked across at her, and when he met her eyes actually blushed too.

Helen retreated when they moved, and began to entertain some of the young ladies; and very soon the Redhurst party were obliged to start to catch their train for Oxley. The parting was cordial on all sides, and Flossy observed to James:

'I did not know you knew the Miss Haywards so well.'

'Oh,' said James, 'I met one of them when she was staying in London, and I came here once to sing at a concert for some schools. They're very nice girls, Flossy— quite in your line—go to Sunday-school, and everything.'

'I daresay,' said Flossy, who did not think this implied a great stretch of virtue.

'And not at all stiff, when you know them.'

'Yes,' said Mrs. Crichton, 'I think I should like to ask two of them over to stay for a few days. I am sure Hugh could not say they were chatterboxes, as he does of the Clintons.'

An indescribably comical expression crossed Jem's face.

'I think it would be a very good plan, mamma,' he said. 'You always get on with *nice* young ladies.'

'Yes, my dear; I get dull by myself,' said Mrs. Crichton, with a sigh. 'Not that we have much amusement to offer them.'

'I don't know that they mind about amusements,' said James.

He was dying for a confidant; for Jem could never keep his affairs to himself, but he did not quite dare to enlighten his mother as to his wishes, for fear she should betray them by over-zeal to the Miss Haywards. It had not quite come to the point of announcing his intentions to Hugh, who would not easily have been convinced of their seriousness. Arthur, who knew the names and charms of most of Jem's many sweethearts, would have been his natural outlet; but how could he tell his love-story to him? Nevertheless, as they sat smoking together that very evening, out it all came—provoked, certainly, by a little joke about the three bouquets; and Arthur was so much amused at the notion of Jem's choice that the latter

was soon absorbed in convincing him that he
had finally made it; which, by his unusual
modesty, he at last succeeded in doing.

'Why, you know, you're irresistible.'

'But *she* never would be attracted by the
same sort of humbug that goes down with
most girls.'

'Oh, come now, Jem, you don't mean to
say so. I don't think I should like her the
better for that.'

'She'd look to what one really was.'

'I'd try a little humbug, though, now
and then.'

Jem laughed.

'I shan't be here when they come, you
see. It's supposed they will suit Hugh; and
he is just the sort of fellow——'

'She'd admire? But, you know, Jem,
Hugh is tolerably safe; and if you came
down on the Saturday we might refer to
your excellences beforehand.'

'I wouldn't say too much,' said Jem,

seriously; then suddenly, ' Arthur, you are a good fellow. It's too bad of me to tell you all this——'

' Don't—don't ! ' interposed Arthur. ' Why should I mind, Jem ? It doesn't make any difference.'

The invitation was sent and accepted by the right pair of sisters, and before they arrived Jem's family had a very good notion of what was expected of them, and were all ready to make the visit pleasant to the young ladies. Arthur divined that Helen, at any rate, was well inclined to be pleased. She was apparently a very good girl, cultivated and intelligent, able to talk on all the subjects expected from a young lady, polite to himself and Hugh, but not particularly in-terested in them. She indulged in a mild but evident enthusiasm for Mrs. Crichton, and made friends with Flossy over school-teaching, books, and favourite heroes ; and she was very pretty and very well dressed.

There was, too, a sort of good-tempered, sunny satisfaction about her, which was not without its charm, especially as the other sister was rather critical of their acquaintances, and Arthur overheard between them the following fragment:

'He goes about smoking on a Sunday afternoon.'

'But he always goes to church again in the evening, Constance.'

'And I don't think, do you, it's *quite* good style to wear that sort of coat?'

'Don't you?'

'A gentleman should have *no* peculiarities.'

'I'm sure, Con, there couldn't be more of a gentleman——'

Here Arthur thought himself bound to retreat, having discovered that the fair Helen could lose her composure sometimes. Jem arrived on the Saturday evening, very much on his best behaviour, and listening to the

Miss Haywards playing the pieces and singing the songs which he had most been wont
to criticise. However, he gave Helen the
names of some new ones, and sang himself,.
as he well knew how to do, contenting himself with finding fault with Freddie's touch..
Hugh did not show off the skill acquired.
under Signor Mattei, which, truth to tell,
was not very considerable.

'I never sing,' he said, emphatically; but.
he sat by and watched, and when some
particular old English ballads were asked
for, and Jem began to wonder where they
were, he checked him quietly, knowing by
Arthur's flush and quiver that they were
among the books which he could not bear to
see touched. Arthur looked grateful, but
Jem found the book on the piano the next
morning.

A slight flaw in the harmony was produced on Sunday afternoon by the discussion
of a new colour, which Miss Constance

Hayward declared to be vulgar, and never worn by any lady ' who was very nice.'

Jem defended it as found in the old masters. It was very artistic.

' I'd rather look like a lady than like a picture,' said Miss Hayward, a little dryly.

' I quite agree with you, Miss Hayward,' said Hugh.

' Hugh's taste *is* conventional usually,' said Jem, in a wicked undertone.

' I *like* that funny green,' said Helen, in her soft, changeless voice, as she rose to get ready for church.

' What makes you laugh so, Arthur ? ' said Hugh, savagely, as they remained for the purpose of taking a walk together, Arthur having a great shrinking from Sunday afternoon at Redhurst.

' I was laughing at Jem. He's fairly caught at last ! '

' Do you mean that this is more than Jem's way ? '

'Oh, yes, and it's coming rapidly to a crisis. Don't you see? I wonder which will rule the roast? Will Jem dress her in "funny green," or will he have to cut his coat according to his lady?'

'It seems to me very unsuitable,' said Hugh, after a slightly-puzzled pause.

'That's the beauty of it, I suppose. One wouldn't have been half so much surprised if Jem had fallen in love with Mademoiselle Mattei!'

'Mademoiselle Mattei had a great many admirers,' said Hugh, as he looked out of window. 'I suppose, now she has recovered her voice, she will fulfil her engagement to that scoundrel—I mean that manager—Vasari.'

'She was very forlorn at the loss of him, poor child,' said Arthur, making most unconscious mischief.

'She told you so?'

'Yes—pretty much. I told her to keep up her heart, and she picked some olive-leaves as a reminder. The other day she told me how she had kept my advice. She is a confiding little creature, and very simple-hearted.'

A silence. Then.

'James is perfectly right to stick to the conventional type—that is, to a known and proved one. Where shall we go this afternoon?'

'Oh, anywhere—I don't care—I think I won't go out,' said Arthur, irresolutely.

'Well, you will have a quiet afternoon,' answered Hugh, glad of the solitude; but even then he paused and retraced his steps.

'Arthur, if this affair of Jem's worries you——'

'Oh, no, no. It gives me something fresh to think about,' said Arthur, with evident truth. 'I'm only—tired.'

'Well, rest then,' said Hugh, with the kind smile that Arthur liked.

Nothing should ever make him thoughtless of Arthur's comfort; but, unsatisfactory as the conversation had been, there was growing up in Hugh's mind the conviction that somehow, somewhere, some when, he would have to ask Violante to tell him the truth.

CHAPTER XXXIX.

PAST AND PRESENT.

' 'Tis time my past should set my future free
For life's renewed endeavour.'

ROSA MATTEI was sitting by herself in her
aunt's drawing-room. That afternoon Violante was expected to arrive from Oxley,
and the next day they would meet Signor
Mattei at the lodging close by, which was to
be their home for the present. It would
not be nearly so pleasant for Rosa as the
ease and companionship of her present quarters ; but she had learnt to accommodate
herself to circumstances, and did not fret
over the prospect of dull evenings. Besides,
it would not be for very long. Rosa's fine,
considerate face rounded into a look of
satisfaction. She had a great deal to tell

Violante and her father. How would they take her news?

'Well, Rosa, sitting and repenting?' said her cousin Beatrice, coming into the room.

'No, Trixy, I'm not going to repent,' said Rosa. 'I'm very well satisfied with my arrangements.'

'I think you are a wise girl, and a lucky girl,' said Miss Grey; 'but I should like to know how you tamed your wild flights down to this result.'

'Well, Beatrice, I never in all my life saw the use of fretting over what can't be helped. It seems to me that the present is just as good a time as the past, and deserves at least as much from one. Things aren't any the better *really* because they happened ever so long ago.'

'Yes. How long have you been so philosophical?'

Rosa blushed, but held her ground.

'When a thing is *impossible* it may be the best thing in itself, but something else may be far better than the shadow of it.'

'"A live dog is better than a dead lion?"'

'Well, yes; now, you see, it was not possible for me to go on the stage, so it was better to put away that, and—and my school-girl fancies with it. I'm not imaginative enough to live on memories, particularly memories of—nothing! And this came——'

'I'm only afraid you might find it a little humdrum——'

'Humdrum, Beatrice? How could it be when Mr. Fairfax is so clever, and so interesting?'

'Ha, ha, Rosy. Come, confess now. This talk is all very well; but you have just gone and fallen in love with Mr. Fairfax, and you'll begin life fresh.'

'If I have I'm afraid it's since I accepted him! I thought—that is, I did not think. But you see, Beatrice, it is not often that a

girl is so fortunate as to meet with anyone——'

'Like him? I'm quite content, Rosy.
You'll do. And now tell me about the prudent part of it.'

'The prudent part is,' said Rosa, 'that he
wishes me to have Violante with me whenever I like—always, if need be. If she gets
on better with father, and if this concert
scheme comes to good, of course that won't
be necessary; but still I shall be able to
take care of her, though she has almost
grown into a woman.'

'I suppose she will go back to school?'

'Oh, yes, I trust so. It is so good for
her. But it is time, I think, that I should
go and meet her.'

Rosa was very happy, and just a little
ashamed of herself for being so. As she had
said, she could not live, and never had lived,
on the memories of her first love; though
circumstances had at times brought them

vividly before her, the very renewal of
them had shown her how entirely they were
vain. Rosa had a very passionate but by no
means a sentimental nature, and both her
common-sense and her craving for a vivid,
happy life forbade her to find satisfaction
in shadowy recollections.

'I am neither silly enough, nor un-
worldly enough,' she thought, as she held
Mr. Fairfax's letter in her hand, and felt that
its offer would be a good exchange for that
bitter old sorrow to which she had offered
up sacrifices enough already.

And, as for that other dream of ambition,
it was tempting, but it was nearly impossible;
and Rosa was a woman and had tried what
earning her living meant, and could guess
pretty well at the taste of the apples of fame,
as well as of the Dead-sea fruits of failure.
And, as Rosa made up her mind to say yes,
she became aware that she was excusing
herself for her readiness to do so, not

arguing against any lurking unwillingness.
It is needless to say that her uncle and
aunt were pleased at her good fortune.
Everyone would be pleased.   And it was
wonderful how well Mr. Fairfax understood
her ideas.   Fancy having Violante to stay with
her in a pretty little house; or, still better,
going with the master of that pretty house
to hear Violante sing and feel proud of her
talents!   It was from such happy visions
that Rosa was roused by the sound of
Violante's voice.

She looked a little paler and graver than
when they had last met, not quite so happy
or so much at her ease; and almost her first
words were :

'I have been singing a great deal, Rosina,
and I think my voice is good.'

'So you have made up your mind to try
to sing again?' said Rosa.

'Yes, Rosina, after the summer I will
come home and sing.'

'You shall not do it if it frightens you and makes you unhappy, my darling.'

'But—father will wish it. And I think everyone is unhappy.'

'My dear child, what makes you take such a gloomy view of life?'

'Why, look, Rosa. Signor Arthur's heart is breaking for his Mysie; while Miss Florence loves him, ah, I know how much!'

'Miss Florence! Does she? I thought her head was full of classes and school-girls.'

'Yes, she will not sit and cry; but I know how she listens when Freddie talks of him, and she will not begin herself to speak of him, but when I ask her questions then she will tell me. She thinks I am only a little girl and know nothing.'

'And you, yourself, dear?'

'I,' said Violante; 'Rosa, I think he is ashamed of having loved me, and that he will never speak to me again.'

'Violante, it is wrong to let you stay there! I shall not consent to it.'

'Ah, no, Rosina, no! *There* I can see that he does not care for me; away, I should think—and hope—and fancy—and—and— oh, let me stay!'

'I am afraid that is not true,' said Rosa, and Violante blushed; for she knew in her heart that Rosa was right.

'*You* look well, Rosina mia,' she said.

'Yes, Violante, I shall surprise you very much. How should you like—you never thought that I—*I* should be engaged to anyone?'

'Rosina *mia!*' exclaimed Violante, with eyes opening wide, and accents of blank astonishment, and then a shower of kisses and questions.

She listened to the story with all the delight that Rosa had anticipated, and after every detail had been discussed between them there was a silence, as Violante sat in her favourite place, leaning against her sister's knee.

'Now,' she said at last, '*now* Rosa, you can tell how hard——'

She paused, and Rosa could hardly help laughing.

'My dear child, I knew that long ago. Listen, Violante, I think it is good for you to know, I was older than you when *my* trouble came, and I think it was as bad as yours. Yet, you see, I am happy.'

'Did you know Mr. Fairfax then?' eagerly said Violante.

'No, no,' said Rosa, 'quite another person. It doesn't signify who he was. It's all gone now.'

'Oh, Rosina, was it when I was a tiresome little girl, and troubled you?'

'You were my one comfort, my darling, never any trouble. But, you see, I told you to show you that one day happiness may

come to you, though quite in a different way
from what you now fancy.'

Violante started up, clasping her hands.
'No, no, Rosina! I will not be happy so!
I would rather have my sorrow. There
would be nothing left in my heart without
it. If he is cruel, he cannot take that
away!'

She spoke so because she was a passionate untaught creature, with instinctive impulses, which she had never learnt to resist.
Yet, did not her lover feel every day the
force of her words; had he not lost with her
the best of himself? Was not Florence,
with all her sense, and all her intellect, re-
signing herself to the same fate? What
would Arthur be without the memory
that was breaking his heart? Her words
awakened an echo strong enough in Rosa's
heart to silence her for the moment.

'If I changed, I should be nothing!' re-
peated Violante.

'You would be what your life had made you, Violante,' said Rosa, 'ready for what might come. And you would want something REAL. But, dear, how should you know anything about it? I should have said the same.'

Violante said no more; but she *thought* that, after all, Rosa's circumstances were different, for *her* unknown lover could never have been like 'Signor Hugo.'

Probably both the girls prepared to meet their father the next day with some trepidation, and as they awaited his arrival they owned to each other that it was very strange to be thinking of supper, and making coffee again.

'It makes me want Maddalena,' said Violante.

'Poor Maddalena! She would not like London fogs. But if I did not make the coffee I am sure there is no one else who could make it fit to drink.'

In due time Signor Mattei arrived, very
affectionate, very voluble, and strangely
familiar to his daughters.

'Ah, my children; how I have pined for
you! While I have been toiling, you have
prospered, and I find you richly clothed;'
here he indicated a piece of new pink
ribbon that was tied round Violante's neck.

'Yes, father,' said Rosa, 'we have some
good news for you, each of us. Will you
have mine first?' and, Signor Mattei assent-
ing, she made her communication, while
Violante sat by wondering how *this* love-
story would be received.

But Signor Mattei was romantic only on
one point.

'He is, no doubt,' he said, 'a fascinating
youth, and respectable, since he is your
uncle's friend; but, figlia mia, his income?
Ah, you cannot live on air!'

'Mr. Fairfax is not a youth, father,' said
Rosa, slightly hurt; 'he is five-and-thirty,

and he has a very good income, which he will explain to you, himself, to-night, if you will allow him. I shouldn't think of living on air.'

Violante had not a strong sense of the ludicrous; but even she could hardly help smiling a little at Rosa's aggrieved air, and could not help wondering how her father would have managed to coerce her resolute, independent sister, even if he had been dissatisfied with ' the fascinating youth's ' prospects, as he replied :

' Then, Rosina, if that point is clear, I will consent.'

' Thank you, father.'

' And will Violante bake a crust of bread for her poor old father when you have left us ? '

' Yes, father. I—I—— My voice is come back. I can sing now.'

Signor Mattei's whole face changed from its sentimental air to a look of fiery enthu-

siasm. He started to his feet, and caught
her hands.

'Your voice, child? All your voice—
every note? Let me hear, let me hear.'

He pulled her towards the piano, which
had been esteemed by Rosa a necessary
part of the furniture of their lodgings,
and, controlling her heart-beating, with a
great effort she sang up and down the scale.
Signor Mattei fairly wept for joy. He kissed
her over and over again, he made her repeat
the notes, he crossed himself, and thanked
the Saints in devouter language than his
daughters had often heard from him; but
finally exclaimed, with an air of chagrin:

'And Vasari has married a woman with
a voice like a screech-owl!'

'That is surely of no consequence,' said
Rosa. 'Violante can never try opera-sing-
ing again. She will never be an actress, and
her health would fail again directly if she

attempted it. But she is willing, after her year at school is over, to try what she can do in the way of concert-singing. And you know that, here in England, no career could be better or more profitable.'

'If you wish it, padre mio,' said Violante, 'I will try now to do what you wish.'

'My sacrifices are repaid!' said Signor Mattei, though he could hardly have defined what the sacrifices were.

The interview with Mr. Fairfax, who shortly arrived, was beyond Rosa's hopes. Violante, though secretly wondering at her sister's taste, could not but be pleased at his kindness, and was forced to acknowledge to herself that, under the most favourable circumstances, she could not have imagined Signor Hugo either condescending to so many explanations, managing to praise exactly the music Signor Mattei liked, or giving quite such a comprehending and

encouraging smile and nod as the one received by Rosa, when her father was a little
argumentative.

Signor Mattei obtained one or two evening engagements, and a good many pupils,
so that Violante did not feel bound to begin
her new life in a hurry; and Rosa began
with a good heart her modest preparations
for the wedding, which was to take place in
the middle of August. The Greys gave a
musical party, at which Signor Mattei played,
and once Mr. Fairfax took them all to the
opera. Rather to Rosa's surprise, Violante
showed no reluctance to make one of the
party. How did she feel when she sat and
looked on at 'Il Don Giovanni,' and saw
another, and how superior, performer playing
her old part of Zerlina? *Her* voice, at its
sweetest and clearest, had never been quite
such as this, and she seemed for the first
time to know what was meant by acting, as

she looked on at the world-famous *prima donna.*

This power, this popularity, this applause was what the father had looked for; the loss of this was what he had mourned. Could she ever have had it, or anything like it? Did she regret now that she could not? Did the woman see the value of what the girl had turned from with tears and distaste? For in this past year, what with trouble, change, and experience, Violante had grown into a woman.

She sat quite still, with her delicate face, pale and passive, and her eyes fixed on the stage. She had pushed all this away from her, all this light and sparkle, this splendour and excitement that had seemed so hard and glaring, so utterly untempting to her shy, tender spirit. What had she gained from that other vision that had worn such a lovely hue? It seemed just then to Violante as if both love and fame had played her false. Since she had lost the first, would it not be better to try and regain the second? It was but a passing thought, but it touched her to the quick. She put out her hand, and held Rosa's tight, as Zerlina curtseyed, and picked up her bouquets.

'Oh,' she thought, 'I would be Zerlina. I would do it all, *all*, if he would throw one. It was better to have all the trouble when he loved me—when he gave me my flowers —my flowers——'

Rosa was not surprised that the old association cost Violante that night such tears as she had not shed for many a month, and Violante wept in silence, uttering no word of her secret yearning and regret.

CHAPTER XL.

PERPLEXITIES.

'Does the road wind up-hill all the way?'

WHILE Violante was in London James
Crichton, at some happy juncture, brought
his wooing to a crisis, and became the
accepted lover of Helen Hayward. His
choice was equally surprising and delightful
to his mother, who threw herself with the
greatest interest into all his preparations for
his marriage in the autumn, invited Helen
whenever her mother would spare her, and
regained all her elastic spirits in this new
interest; while James smiled more than ever,
and talked about Helen to everyone who
would listen. Both his cousin and his brother

were naturally strongly affected by this new
love-story working itself out beside them.
Lengthening days, summer weather, summer
flowers, and summer habits, could not but
remind both of them of what these young
days of last year had been to them. There
awoke in Hugh all the old questioning with
himself; all the old arguments that he had
thought laid at rest for ever; all the old
passion, which jealousy and self-reproach
had for the time overclouded. He hardly
knew how; but his belief in the causes which
he had for jealousy had gradually faded, and
he no longer believed that Violante was
either engaged to the manager or that she
was pining for his loss. A little reflection
convinced him that all that Arthur had told
him of her sadness *might* have been caused
by the memory of himself, and something in
the look of her eyes at their two brief meet-
ings confirmed this thought. As Hugh's
mind gradually freed itself from the hard,

bitter judgment of himself and of others that had followed the stern self-reproach and self-pity which had for so long occupied it, as his new kindliness towards Arthur warmed and softened him, he came to view things in a more natural light, and ceased to tell himself that his love, like everything else, was turned to bitterness. No, it was sweet and soft and strong as in the May-days of last year; but Hugh had become far more conscious of the difficulties attending it, and Hugh had lost in this year of sorrow and self-distrust the bounding energy by which he had intended to overcome them. Besides, he was no longer quite the authority that he had been at home, and, though Violante was doubtless really more fitted to marry him by her school-life, she had lost a great advantage in having become known first to his mother as a girl whom there was not the slightest likelihood of his fancying. A wonderful Italian unknown beauty was one thing; a little foreign, penniless girl, half-singer, half-school-teacher, was quite another. And though Hugh was, of course, his own master, his relations to his family formed so large a part of his life that he hardly knew how to disturb them, and the Crichtons belonged to exactly the class most easily disturbed by an incongruous marriage. He had given up the notion that he ought to punish himself for the destruction of Arthur's happiness by destroying his own; but his feelings strongly revolted against any deliberate effort to secure it just at the time then coming, and there was nothing morbid in the belief that he was bound to make Arthur his first consideration; for Arthur's sake, not for that of his own conscience. And what was to become of Arthur was a problem that grew in difficulty.

The recurrence of these once happy summer days, perhaps spite of himself, Jem's bright hopes, and the return to the amusement and occupations of which Mysie had been the centre, were more than he could bear, and cost him such heart-sickness as he had never yet known.

It seemed as if his light-hearted youth had been beaten at last in the struggle, and efforts to brave it out only made matters worse ; and, though he had, perhaps, never fought so hard with himself, he got none of the credit that had attached to his first home-coming. They did not cease to pity him for his sorrow, but it did become wearisome to sympathise with the indications of it, and it was impossible to order matters only with reference to him. He was out of place among them, and he felt it keenly, yet he could not resolve to go away by himself. He had grown very reserved, and certainly tried as much as possible to avoid notice ; and even Hugh, who saw the most of him, found it very difficult to know how to deal with him, and turned over many plans in his mind, none of which appeared to him quite satisfactory.

They were walking home together one afternoon by the field-path from Oxley. The summer heat was beginning to be felt in the air, the summer look was coming over the woods and fields. The summer silence would soon succeed to the perpetual song and twitter of the birds. They were walking on silently, when, tripping down the path came a smartly-dressed girl, with fair hair flying. It was Alice Wood, who had been absent all the year. As she recognised them, she started violently and stopped, a sudden look of agitation in her face as she made a half-curtsey.

Arthur hesitated, then went up rather eagerly, and shook hands with her.

'How d'ye do—you have been away?' he said.

'Yes, sir, at my aunt's, learning dress-making. I—I hope you are pretty well, Mr. Arthur,' she added, faltering.

Arthur seemed unable to say more ; he turned away from her, and she hurried on, crying as she went.

The two young men stood still, each of them overpowered by the sight of her. Then Hugh saw that Arthur shivered, and was very pale. He turned towards a tree-trunk near, and sat there with hidden face, trying to recover himself, while all Hugh's agony of remorse once more came over him.

'God knows, Arthur, I wish the stroke had fallen on me!' he said. 'It is from *me* you should shrink. How can you bear the sight of *me!*'

Arthur did not answer, but he looked up after a few minutes, and said simply :

'I am very sorry. I wish I could get over these things.'

'This was not a thing to be got over.'

'No. But, Hugh, the canal—the meadows—it's like a nightmare—I can't forget them. I have tried to go there—to conquer

it, but I never could.   Yet I have dreamt
over and over again of it.'

'You never spoke of this?' said Hugh.

'Oh, no.   Hugh, have you ever been
there?'

'Yes,' said Hugh, 'often at first.   It was
better than thinking of it.'

'Will you come with me, and get it
done?   I think I could—with you.'

'Oh, my dear boy, I don't think I ought
to let you do that.'

'It would be over.   But I don't
know——   In the morning, when it looks
different.'

'Yes, not now,' said Hugh, firmly.   'See
here, Arthur.   I have guessed at these
feelings of yours.   I know too well how
natural and inevitable they are.   But Redhurst is no fit place for you just now, and I
have a plan.   Should you like to come back
to the Bank House and stay there with me?
I think it's comfortable, and you could rest,

and there would be no discussions about society, and no worries. If you *could* like to be alone with me?'

'I should like it very much,' said Arthur, decidedly. 'I know I'm no good at home, but I cannot bear the thought of wandering about.'

'Well, then, shall we come back now? You are tired and shaken, and I will go and explain things at home.'

'Yes. Hugh, we shan't rake up all these matters again ; but I want to tell you, once for all, that you mistook my feeling about yourself. I need not say I never blamed you—how could I? But all this nervous folly can only belong to—to indifferent objects. You suffered too, only at first I could not think of that. But you *do* help me—you always know the right thing for me.'

'I would lay down my life for you,' said Hugh, passionately.

'No. But you will help me to recover myself. I'm glad I have told you. And as for what must remain, when—when I have "got over it," as they say—life without her —though you wouldn't think it after this, I believe I am learning to look forward to it a little better, and I shall have you to help me.'

'I have been very miserable about it,' said Hugh, moved to equal simplicity by Arthur's straightforwardness. 'It was my first comfort when you said I helped you. Nothing shall ever come between us : you shall be my first thought, for ever.'

Hugh's voice swelled and quivered ; he did nothing but hold Arthur's hand for a moment, but no sign or gesture of passionate emotion would have seemed exaggerated to his feeling then. 'I *can* make atonement,' he thought.

Arthur, who, after all, cared far less about the relations between them, though his

affectionate expressions had been perfectly
genuine, said more lightly :

'Then are we to turn back to Oxley?'

'Yes ; then you will not have to talk it
all over at home ; I'll settle it.'

So they retraced their steps ; and Hugh
took Arthur into the Bank House and upstairs, where he had never been for years.
It was rather a large house, in the time of
their grandfather the largest in Oxley, and was
well-furnished and handsome. The drawing-
room had never been used by Hugh ; but
he had established himself in the library,
a stiff, old-fashioned room, with two long,
narrow windows, with high window-seats in
them. His writing-table, with its untidy
masculine papers, had intruded on the orderly
arrangements in which his grandmother, who
had long survived her husband, had delighted. Arthur sat down in one of the
window-seats while Hugh gave the orders rendered necessary by this unexpected decision.

'Do you remember how we used to come here to see grandmamma?' he said.

'Yes, but I should have thought you were too small to recollect it.'

'I remember it, perfectly. You used to be desired to keep Jem and me from walking on the grass; and you obeyed implicitly!'

'You may walk on the grass now, if you like,' said Hugh.

'It was a nice old garden. And, I declare, Hugh, there are the cats!'

'Cats? I haven't got a cat.'

'The velvet cats on the mantelpiece—the first works of art I ever appreciated.'

And he pointed out two cats cut out in black velvet, and painted into tortoiseshell, with fierce eyes and long whiskers, objects of delight to the infant mind of any generation.

'I declare I never noticed them. You had better find out some more old friends, while I go over to Redhurst.'

The experiment proved very successful

on both sides. It gave Arthur the rest he
needed; the absence of association without the
strain of novelty. His cheerfulness revived ;
and, perhaps, Hugh had rarely found life
more pleasant: for, though he was tenderly
desirous of making his cousin comfortable,
of saving him fatigue, and amusing without
oppressing him, it was really Arthur who
twisted the things about till the room looked
homelike and cheerful; found out how cool and
shady the garden was, and how pretty a few
changes might make it, and started agreeable
subjects of conversation. Though not so
amusing and argumentative as Jem, he was
a wonderfully pleasant person to live with,
even when languid and only half himself;
and Hugh, delighted to find that the companionship suited Arthur, grew quite lively
himself under its influence. They saw
James whenever he came to Oxley, and
frequently Mrs. Crichton; and Hugh dutifully
went over, at short intervals, to Redhurst,

and, though he avoided without regret many
summer gaieties, was obliged to share in a
few, and, among others, went to a large
musical party given by Mrs. Dysart.

There had been some croquet and archery
in the afternoon; but Hugh did not make
his appearance till just as the music was going
to begin.

'How late you are, Hugh!' said his.
mother, as he came up and joined her. 'And
no Arthur?'

'No; he was tired with the heat. I never
meant to let him come. I am sure I'm early
enough. They're just going to begin.'

And Hugh sat down by his mother, and
listened decorously to an instrumental piece.
It was still early, some of the company were
still wandering in the gardens, and the windows were open, letting in the soft evening
air. But some wax candles were lighted at
one end of the drawing-room, where the
performers were gathered, and as Hugh, after

listening to one or two songs and to a violin solo, was politely suppressing a yawn, a young lady stepped into the light. It was Violante— Violante, the same as when she had stood in the hot Italian sunlight, and sung to her father's pupils. The same, and yet different. It seemed to Hugh's confused eyes that she had turned into a fashionable lady, in her trailing white muslin, with its puffs and flounces, with her soft, curling hair, done up in an attempt at the prevailing fashion. She looked taller, older somehow—more unmistakably a beauty ; but not, he thought, at first—his own Violante. She held her head up too, and if she was frightened managed to conceal it. Hugh made a snatch at his mother's programme.

'Who—what—how?'

'Don't you know?' said Clarissa Venning, who was near them. 'Miss Mattei's voice has come back. I suppose she will sing again in public ; but *this* you know is quite

in a private capacity. She was asked to come
with Florence.'

Hugh looked at the programme:—' Song.
—Miss Violante Mattei.'

He was just about to commit himself to a
vehement exclamation of astonishment that
no one had thought of telling him she was
going to sing—how could they overlook
such a fact ?—when the old, sweet notes
fell again on his ear, as lovely as ever he
thought, and he listened, breathless, till they
ceased amid loud applause and exclamations
of admiration.

Violante smiled and curtseyed her thanks,
with elaborate grace, and as no young lady
amateur would have thought of doing.

' She has such pretty foreign manners,'
cried a lady ; and one of the young men of
the house, laughing, tossed her a little bunch
of flowers, and she picked it up and curtseyed
again, just as she had been taught to do by

old Madame Cellini, long ago in Civita Bella.

She was to sing once again, and Hugh waited in breathless expectation; but though the applause was as ardent as ever, she only acknowledged it this time by a dignified little bow, and retreated.

'Oh,' said one of the Dysarts, 'someone has been telling her her pretty curtsey was not *selon les règles*. What a shame!'

'She is a very beautiful girl,' said Mrs. Crichton, who, now that there was no need to fear Jem's foolishness, was ready to be interested in Violante.

'Yes,' said Clarissa. 'She is too fine a bird for us, which is a pity, as she is a nice little thing; and never so happy as when she is playing with the little ones. Ah, here she comes!'

Violante came up to Clarissa, without immediately perceiving her companions.

'Miss Clarissa, Miss Florence says they

arc going to dance. May we stay a little
longer?'

'No one could think of carrying you
away, Miss Mattei,' said Mr. Dysart. 'Pray,
let me thank you for your songs. And,
of course, Miss Venning, you are not thinking
of stirring yet? Let me find you a partner.'

'Thank you, I am acting chaperone.
You may stay if Florence likes, Violante.
I think you have not seen Mrs. Crichton'?

' Let me thank you for your sweet music,
my dear,' said Mrs. Crichton, in her kind
way. 'I think it was my other son you
knew in Italy?'

'Mother, you mistake. It was I. I knew
Mademoiselle Mattei *once*.' And Hugh started
forward and held out his hand, imploringly.
Violante put hers into it; but she stood
passive and still.

' You were not so gracious, Miss Mattei,
when we applauded you the second time,'
said young Mr. Dysart.

'I saw that the young ladies did not curtsey, signor,' said Violante, simply; 'but I thank you for listening to me.'

As she spoke the lights flashed up and revealed her standing, facing Hugh, with a sort of desperate self-possession, as the first notes of the dance-music sounded.

'Mr. Crichton, I think you don't dance. Miss Mattei, will you give me this waltz?' said another Dysart, approaching.

Violante was no coquette, but she was a woman, and her pride had been hurt by Hugh's neglect. So she smiled graciously, and moved away as Florence joined them, before Hugh could get out a somewhat undignified and hurried declaration that he did dance—sometimes.

'We must only stay for three dances,. Flossy,' said Clarissa.

But Violante had promised the three dances before she had left their side five minutes; and Hugh returned home, with

the discovery that he was not the only man
of taste in the world, and the firm conviction that Violante was wholly indifferent to
him. It is also remarkable that at the same
time he forgot entirely all the excellent arguments by which he had endeavoured to render
himself indifferent to her.

CHAPTER XLI.

THUNDER-SHOWERS.

'But whither would my fancy go ?
How out of place she makes
The violet of a legend blow
Among the chops and steaks!'

AFTER Mrs. Dysart's party there ensued a
fortnight of intensely hot weather ; so close
and sultry that it wore a shade or two of
pink even off Flossy's rosy cheeks and ac-
counted partly for Violante's demeanour
being unusually languid and *distraite*.

Mrs. Crichton had gone to London to
superintend some of James' preparations and
Frederica had been left at Oxley Manor, so
nothing, of course, was heard there of the

young men at the Bank House. It seemed
to poor Flossy as if, with the discovery of
her new feelings for Arthur their old intercourse had vanished away, for on his removal to Redhurst, she ceased to see him,
and she could not feel that she counted for
anything in his life. Thus separated from
him, she felt with and for him every pang
of memory and association more keenly
than he always felt them for himself.

Poor Flossy! To have given her affection not only without thought of return, but
to one lying under such a heavy cloud of
trouble, was enough to tame her exuberant
brightness ; and her lessons lost their liveliness, her own occupations their interest.
Miss Venning might have seen that something was amiss; but she was greatly
occupied in receiving the two little sons of
the brother just older than Clarissa, who
had been settled in India for some time; and,
if she thought Flossy looking pale, merely

suggested a holiday visit to the eldest brother, who was a Lancashire clergyman, or observed that the care of the little boys would make a nice change for her. Flossy was too young to have had much home intercourse with any of her brothers, and not just then in the humour to take up with anything new.

But Clarissa had never been so fond of anyone as of the brother Walter, whose youthful scrapes and youthful interests had all been confided to her ear, and whose departure for India had been the great grief of her girlhood.

'What a blessing they're not girls!' was her comment on the letter announcing their arrival.

'Indeed!' said Miss Venning. 'It would be easier to do for them here if they were.'

'Oh, I daresay they'll fit in,' said Clarissa. 'We want a little change.'

And she went herself to Southampton to fetch them, and took them silently under her special protection, making exquisite and ever-varying grimaces for their amusement and jealous of the character of their favourite aunt. Miss Venning was glad that the children were so well provided for, and Flossy perceived that Clarissa had at last found an interest in life.

One sultry afternoon early in July Flossy, with Violante and two or three elder girls, had been to a lecture which had been held in Oxley by some celebrated personage. Miss Venning had taken the opportunity of paying a visit and had desired them to meet her at a certain shop in the town. As they crossed the market-place ominous sounds were heard and heavy drops began to fall.

'We're going to have a thunderstorm,' said Flossy, looking up at the bank of heavy clouds that was rolling up.

' Oh, Miss Florence, what shall we do ? ' said Violante, rather timidly.

' My new hat ! ' exclaimed one girl.

' It's going to pour,' said another.

' We must run across to the station,' said Flossy, ' or down to Cooper's, as my sister said.'

As they stood for a moment hesitating which way to turn, they were suddenly accosted.

' Flossy ! There's going to be a great storm. Come in with me. You will all be wet through,' and Arthur hurried up to them.

' The station—Mary,' murmured Flossy.

' The station ? Nonsense ! you'll all be drenched. I'll send after Miss Venning. Come, Flossy, don't drown your flock from a sense of propriety. I'm sure Mademoiselle Mattei doesn't like thunder.'

The gay voice, the familiar address, chased away half Flossy's fears and senti-

ments. She laughed and yielded, and they
hurried through the plashing rain-drops
across the road and into the Bank House—
unknown ground to them all.

'Come upstairs,' said Arthur, and he
led the way into his grandmother's drawing-room, into which for the sake of coolness
he had lately penetrated.

The delighted schoolgirls gathered into
a knot, smiling and whispering. Violante
glanced round, as in sacred precincts, and
Arthur, pointing to the lashing rain, laughed
boyishly.

'Here you are, fairly caught in the
ogre's castle. What shall I do—shall I have
up Mrs. Stedman?'

'Don't be so absurd,' said Flossy, aside.
'What will the girls think of you?'

'No? Then I'll try to be polite. Isn't
this a quaint room, Miss Mattei?'

It was a long room with three high
windows, looking over the garden, against

which the rain was beating violently. Everything was slender, prim, and pale-coloured. Old-fashioned prints hung on the walls, on the paper of which long-tailed birds drank out of wonderful vases. Old china was varied by wax flowers and queer little bits of fancy work. Elaborate wool-work chairs were preserved with tight-fitting muslin covers. Arthur made Violante sit down in a tall straight-backed one; he opened a cabinet of curiosities for the amusement of the girls, and was just beginning: 'I don't know when I've seen you, Flossy,' when the door opened and Hugh walked in, to find the stiff grandmotherly chamber full of laughing, summer-clothed girls, and in the centre, soft and smiling, Violante herself.

'Hugh looks like a man who has ridden into a fairy ring,' said Arthur, as his cousin paused in utter surprise.

Hugh made a few polite speeches, Flossy

some rather hurried explanations, and then
their host fell silent, till, after a minute or
two, he said, gravely :

'Arthur, don't you think we could give
these young ladies some tea ? '

'To be sure. I'll go and see what can
be produced.'

'Arthur has made the house quite habit-
able,' said Hugh to Flossy.

'He looks much better than when I saw
him last.'

'Yes, I think he is better; but he has
felt the hot weather, and he always turns the
brightest side up, you know.'

Hugh's affectionate tone turned up quite
a new side of himself to Flossy ; but Violante
recognised the familiar accents which she
had missed so sorely at first. He did not
speak a word to her; but her heart was
beating, she felt intensely happy.

Arthur presently reappeared, followed
by Mrs. Stedman, with preparations for tea
and such a plentiful supply of cakes of all

descriptions as Flossy suspected had cost the office-boy a wetting to obtain from the neighbouring pastry-cook's. The girls were in a state of blissful delight. Was there ever such a fortunate thunder-shower? and, perhaps, their young teachers were not far from the same opinion.

'I'm afraid it's going to clear up,' whispered one of the younger ones.

'There's not a chance of it,' said Arthur, gravely. 'It's going to pour for an hour yet.' But struggling sunbeams began to force their way through the clouds and to dance on the rain-drops. Arthur flung up the window and a great rainbow was arching over the sky, while trees, grass, and flowers were brilliant with reflected light.

It *had* cleared up, and Miss Venning made her appearance in her friend's water-proof cloak, with—

'Well, young ladies, I need not have been anxious about your getting wet!'

'You're just in time to have some tea, Miss Venning,' said Arthur. 'They were just getting wet through when I met them.'

Miss Venning drank her tea, and carried off her flock; but, though no one had exchanged a word in private, somehow that tea-drinking had left three people much happier than it found them.

It seemed to have restored to Flossy a natural intercourse with Arthur, and to have brought his real self before her again; while to Violante it had restored the gentle, smiling Signor Hugo of last year. The effect on Hugh was less definite, but it was long since he had laughed so much as at Arthur's account of his finding the girls hesitating and wondering in the fast-coming rain.

He was engaged the next morning for some time by a meeting at which the plans for the gas-works, which had been invested with so incongruous an interest, and the plans for the new railway were brought forward and discussed, and it was with a very grave face that he came back to Arthur with some papers in his hand.

'Look, Arthur,' he said. 'I must show you what has been proposed about this rail-road. You know they want to connect Fordham and Oxley, and the line proposed would cut right through the Ashenfold woods and along the bed of the canal (which would not be worth keeping up if there was a railroad), and keep by the bank of the river up to the 'Pot of Lilies' and then strike across the heath to Fordham. Redhurst would have a station somewhere down by the lock. This is much the most direct line ; but it is possible that they might take one round at the back of the woods, and as the property nearly all belongs to my mother we might, perhaps, get it adopted. I want to know how it strikes you.'

Hugh made this long, business-like explanation without pausing, and now he drew the plan forward and pointed out the proposed route.

' It *shall* not be done if you mind it very much,' he said, vehemently, as there was no answer.

' Does Aunt Lily know ? ' said Arthur.

' Yes. She is not unwilling. I would not have it talked of till it was necessary to tell you about it.'

' I remember it was talked of once before. We thought it dreadful destruction ; but you said then that a good many local interests were involved in it, that it would be a good thing for the place, and that it would be a very unpopular act to oppose it.'

' I don't care a straw about the unpopularity,' said Hugh.

' What, when you know you're the Member of the future ? No, Hugh ; what reason could you give for opposing it ? Don't vex yourself about me. Why should one cling to the mere empty shell of things? To oppose a real public advantage for—for our feelings. It would just be ridiculous, and can't be done. You would be the first to say so.'

This was perfectly true; yet Hugh could as little bear to hear the effort in Arthur's voice as if he had not been a sensible, clear-headed man of business, who scorned the notion of acting on sentimental motives. For his own part the removal of all these haunted places was a positive relief; but he knew that to Arthur it was like rifling a grave.

'When is this likely to be carried out?' said Arthur, presently.

'Why, very soon—if they get it through Parliament before the end of the session. To-day is the fifteenth of July——'

Arthur started up and walked away to the window. Was the fate of the poor old

'Pot of Lilies' to be sealed on the very day of
the year when, with such mirth and· merry-
making, they had agreed to revisit it and
renew their innocent little celebration ; to
live over once more the hours that had
been so cloudless and so gay? Ah, never,
never again !

There came over Arthur one of those
agonies of regret that were worse to bear
than any nervous horror, even than the daily
loneliness to which he was trying to grow
accustomed.   He seemed to feel again
Mysie's little hand in his ; to see her sweet
round eyes looking into his own. The air
was sweet again with summer fragrance ; the
sun shone hot and clear in as blue a sky ; but
that hand—those eyes—— He hurried away,
and Hugh dared not follow him, and, having
no mental picture of the daily events of the
past summer till it had broken up into storm
and misery, could not tell what had affected
him so strongly.

He could only try to be doubly tender and considerate, and, as soon as he thought Arthur could bear any discussion about himself, suggested that they should go together for a little trip to North Wales. He had not been away himself for more than a year, and could easily contrive to take the holiday. His mother, he knew, meant to go to the sea almost immediately; so Redhurst would be shut up, and Oxley was too hot and dusty in August to be endurable. Arthur acquiesced, rather languidly, but as if he knew it was right.

'Jem asked me if I would like to take a last bachelor trip with him; but I should have known all the time that his heart was elsewhere,' he said.

'You will not think I want to be anywhere else,' said Hugh, and, perhaps, just at that time he hardly did.

The trip prospered. Arthur was fond of travelling and clever in contriving plans for it. He was grave and quiet as Hugh had never known him, with fewer ups and downs of spirits, and seemed to be losing the boyishness that had clung to him so obstinately; and so the dreaded days drew near, with nothing whatever to mark their coming, and the first Sunday in August dawned damp and grey over heathery hills and mossy valleys. They were at a place where there was no English service. Arthur went to hear the Welsh one, and Hugh wandered about, anxious and wretched, and yet with his mind perversely filled with hopeful visions of Violante. He would have liked to make this a day of penance, but whenever he let his mind loose, as it were, it sprang back like an elastic band to the image that daily filled it more and more.

'It has not been at all a bad day, Hugh,' said Arthur, gently, as they parted for the night. 'I am glad we came here. To-morrow, if you will, we'll go for a long walk somewhere.'

And so they spent that Monday, so full of memories—though, of course, the Tuesday was the real anniversary of Mysie's death—beneath cool, dull skies, over hill-sides half shrouded in mountain mists, heather and furze for roses and carnations, cloud for sunshine, wild lonely solitudes for homely quiet. They did not talk very much; but the day had none of the terror that Hugh had anticipated from it. Rather it had a kind of sorrowful peace.

In the afternoon the mist thickened into heavy rain; and, as they approached a small wayside public-house, Hugh suggested that they should take shelter; find out exactly where they were, and if there was any chance of a conveyance to Beddgelert, where they had ordered their luggage to meet them. They had been walking all day, and if their

object had been to look at the scenery,
instead of to find some monotonous occupation,
would have been much disappointed.

Accordingly they turned into the little
inn, and while Hugh went to enquire of an
English-speaking host as to the possibility
of reaching Beddgelert, Arthur, who had
picked up a few words of Welsh, and
generally contrived to make himself understood, was engaged in a lively pantomime
with the tall, dark-eyed girl who waited
on them, making her laugh and talk volubly
and incomprehensibly, as he tried to indicate
that he wanted something hot to drink, and
something substantial to eat. There was no
guest-room but the low, spacious kitchen
into which they had first entered, and he
was standing before the smouldering peat
fire and pointing with animated gestures
first to the bottle and then to his flask when
the house door was burst open, and a whole
party of tourists, struggling with wind, water-

proofs and umbrellas, ran hastily in. There
were three ladies and two gentlemen, and
they were too much occupied in shaking
themselves free from their wraps to perceive
Arthur, till Hugh came back, saying:
'There's nothing to be got here, Arthur,'
when a young lady, letting her water-
proof drop on the floor, sprang forward.
'Why, it's Mr. Spencer Crichton! How
d'ye do?—oh, how funny! Charlie, Charlie,
here's Mr. Crichton!'

'Miss Tollemache!' exclaimed Hugh, in
equal surprise, as Emily Tollemache, bright-
haired, frank-faced, and smiling, stood confused, while her brother came forward
with—

'Why, Crichton, who in the world would
have thought of meeting you here?'

One or two letters had passed between
Hugh and Mr. Tollemache since their parting; but with no reference to the past, the
restraint of which had caused each to be

less inclined to seek out the other, and
Arthur, as Hugh made a sort of introduction
of his friends, could not fail to be struck by
his look of embarrassment. Emily, however,
was equal to the occasion.

'So, you see, Mr. Crichton, we *have* come
to England, and I do like it so much, quite
as much as I expected. Mamma is in London,
and we are travelling with my cousins, only
it has rained every day since we came here.'

'Our climate certainly is variable,' said
Hugh.

'I am afraid you must regret Italian
sunshine, Miss Tollemache,' put in Arthur,
as he tried to kick the peats into a blaze.

'Oh, no! not yet. But it seems quite
natural to see Mr. Crichton. And you know
we went away and I have never seen Rosa
or my dear Violante. I wonder what has
become of them!'

'I can tell you that,' said Hugh, and
Arthur saw Mr. Tollemache turn and look

at him with an involuntary start; while
Hugh grew crimson, as he continued: 'They
came to England, and she went, by chance,
to school at Oxley.'

'How strange! Do you ever see her?
Oh, what a lovely, dear creature she was
when we all went to the classes together!
Did *you* ever see her?' to Arthur—'Couldn't
I find her out?'

Arthur answered with a few words of
explanation as to Violante's present circumstances, but he felt as if he were finding the
explanation of all sorts of trifles which
he had thought strange, but had been too
much preoccupied to reason about.

'Mamma wants me to go to school,' said
Emily, 'and, though I consider myself much
too old, I should like to go to school with
Violante.'

Here Mr. Tollemache changed the conversation decidedly, and Hugh said aside to
Arthur:

'This is very unlucky! That we should
have encountered all these people! Cannot
we get away?'

Arthur glanced expressively at the
window, against which the mountain-rain
was beating almost in sheets of water.

'It cannot be helped,' he said, 'and I do
not mind it.'

He had only meant to reassure Hugh's
anxiety for him; but he was surprised at the
colour and hurry with which Hugh dis-
claimed minding it on his own account. So
they were obliged to stay and eat fried ham
and eggs together; and Arthur, by cultivating
Miss Tollemache's acquaintance discovered a
good deal that was new about Hugh's visit
to Civita Bella, and by the time their meal
was over the clouds had lifted, and the
Tollemaches' carriage, which they had left
some two or three miles behind them for the
sake of the mountain walk, came in search of
them. Hugh and Arthur found that they

were only five or six miles from Beddgelert;
and after Hugh had extorted from himself an
invitation to the Tollemaches to come to
Redhurst, which he was sure that his mother
would follow up, and had parted cordially
with his friends, they set forth on their walk
once more alone together.

CHAPTER XLII.

THE MEETING OF THE WATERS.

'And the brooklet has found the billow,
    Though they flowed so far apart,
And has filled with its passionate sweetness
    That turbulent, bitter heart.'

THE heavy walls of mist slowly lifted themselves, and the purple mountain-sides showed
dark and close at hand. The passionate rush
of the mountain torrents sounded full and
free after the violent rain, and their foam
showed white against the grass and heather,
ready to dance in the first rays of returning
sunshine. Arthur and Hugh walked on for
some distance in silence—a silence that confirmed Arthur's suspicions. It was so strange
a revelation, so much in contrast with his

life-long surface knowledge of Hugh's character, that he hesitated to believe it. Yet
all Violante's looks and sayings, which he
had understood as referring to Vasari, were
now, he perceived, capable of another inter-
pretation. He now recollected his impression that there had been something amiss
with Hugh on his first return from Italy, the
passing thought that had flashed across him
when he had seen them together at the
primrose-picking ; Violante's wish to go to
England, and her content when she found
herself there ; and, more than all, Hugh's
flushed, agitated look as he walked on
now beside him.

'Hugh,' said Arthur, with sudden courage, 'I think I have found the clue to a
great deal that has puzzled me. I thought
it was the manager-lover for whom Violante
was fretting at Caletto. I think now——'

'What do you mean? Fretting? You
told me it was Vasari—you confirmed all
my suspicions. Tell me the real truth, what

was it?' cried Hugh, stopping suddenly, and facing round upon him.

'I made mischief, I am afraid,' said Arthur, 'but I had a preconceived idea. I see now that her hints and her little sorrowful ways were on your account only. How *could* I guess *you* had anything to do with her?'

'Don't laugh at me!' cried Hugh, fiercely.

'I don't want to laugh. I want you to tell me the whole story.'

'Tell *you*—now?' said Hugh, recollecting himself. 'No, no, impossible.'

'You can't leave me in such a state of conjecture. Here, it's quite fine and sunny now. Let us stop by this stile, and tell me all about it.'

As he spoke Arthur perched himself on the stone step of the stile, while Hugh leaned against the wall beside him. The white masses of cloud torn in every direction rolled rapidly away, showing great wells of blue

between them. Every stone and puddle
shone and sparkled in the sunshine ; sharp
peaks, and large, round masses of rock came
one by one into view.

In this unfamiliar scene, to the last person
and at the last moment that he could possibly have anticipated, Hugh began to tell
his story. Arthur listened with a few well-
timed questions, till Hugh spoke of ' trying
to convince Jem,' when he could not repress
a laugh.

' Jem in the seat of judgment ! '

Hugh laughed too, and went on, more
comfortably :

' He said nothing I did not know before.
I meant to carry it through. I could have
done so.'

' Then you did not come to an explanation with her ? '

' Yes, I did. I thought *then* I had found
out the secret of life,' said Hugh, with an
intensity of feeling, which Arthur could
well sympathise with.

'But what on earth upset it all?'

'Didn't I see her with the diamonds, taking them from him?—ah!' Hugh broke off, and drove his heel into the ground, unable to recall the scene without passion that was almost uncontrollable, and turning white with the effort to restrain language and gesture to the dry composure which he had adopted.

'Her father said she was already engaged to him,' he said, after a pause; then hurried on with his story, and demanded:

'Now, what do you say to that?'

'That I would not have believed you could be such a fool,' would have been Arthur's natural answer, but he modified it into, 'Well, I think you were very hasty, and rather hard on the poor child——'

'Hard? Do you think I was hard— don't you think I was justified in what I did?'

'I don't think you allowed enough for her father's authority and her own timidity —certainly.'

' Sometimes I think I acted like a brute,' said Hugh.

' Well, but you see the worse you acted the less you were deceived in *her*,' said Arthur, plainly. ' Well, then you came home and thought it was all over ? '   .

' Yes. Perhaps you can understand now what caused the temper and the conduct which led to—to—. Could I have had *any* conscience, *any* feeling, and have renewed *my* happiness after last year ? '

' But how was it ? ' said Arthur, hardly comprehending a view so unlike his own instincts.

' Well, you know recent circumstances as well as I do. I have become aware that, however it may have been once—I think now she is not indifferent to me, but I saw all the difficulties more plainly—that was not it, she is more than all the world to me—but *how* could I do it ? '

' But, Hugh,' said Arthur, gently, ' what

good could it possibly do me for you to make yourself miserable ? '

' No good,' said Hugh. ' I know that now. But I could bear better to see you. I should have hated my own happiness.'

Arthur did not answer for a moment. He was thinking how little they had any of them known of Hugh.

' But you make me out rather a dog in the manger,' he said, with a half-smile.

' No, no ! You are all that is unselfish. But I was not thinking of you. I know I was mistaken, but lately I have seen things differently.'

' It has been a great comfort to me to have you to look after me lately,' said Arthur, with tact to say the most soothing thing ; ' and, no doubt, last year you did not know what you felt. But I should not have thought you heartless. There is one person whose feelings I think you have forgotten— Violante herself.'

'When I believed she loved me it seemed too good a thing for me to put out my hand to take,' said Hugh, in a low voice.

'Oh, Hugh,' said Arthur, sadly and earnestly, 'don't throw away a great love. Neither she nor you will ever most likely feel the like again. It is much too good to lose. It's the best thing in the world, you know.'

'And I must have it. *I*, while *you*——' said Hugh, with much agitation.

'You *have* it. She loves you, and you only can make her happy.'

'You don't imagine,' said Hugh, passionately, 'that I don't know how precious, how utterly good it is! You don't think I don't love her?'

'No, no, I don't think that.'

There was a moment's silence, and then Hugh said, more lightly:

'And how about my mother, and all that part of the business?'

'As to that, Jem was right, of course, at
an early stage of the proceedings; but it is
not such an extreme case but what I think it
may all be managed. Violante is differently
placed now, and is herself all anyone could
wish. And you wouldn't be worth much
without her, Hugh.'

'Just nothing,' said Hugh.

'Well, then,' said Arthur, boldly, 'why
don't you go home to-morrow morning and
see her?'

Hugh leant over the wall in silence,
enduring a conflict of feeling that only such
natures ever know. He desired this thing
with passionate intensity; he knew, from
bitter experience, that he could not bear its
loss. He was not one whose feet went cre-
ditably along the paths of self-denial, or
from whom voluntary self-sacrifice came with
any grace. And yet he felt how little he
deserved this blessing, how utterly beyond
his merits it would be, with such humiliation
that he could hardly bear to put out his

hand to take it. To feel himself crowned with such undeserved joy, to take it almost from Arthur's hand—to find that there was left for him no expiation, no penance even for the wrong he had done—to know ' that no man may deliver his brother, nor make agreement unto God for him,' was a pang unknown to humbler, simpler souls, but bitter as death to him.

It was almost inconceivable to Arthur, with his unconquerable instinct for making the best of things, and his readiness to accept consolation from any quarter. He had no particular insight into character, nor any inclination to sit in judgment on his neighbours; but he did perceive that Hugh was distressed by the contrast between their fortunes, and that he was suffering under an access of self-reproach, so he said :

'You can't tell how much good you have done me lately. It has been the greatest rest to be with you; but this will only be pleasure to me. I know you would put it all off to save me any pain, but I shall be happier for it—I shall indeed—don't have a single scruple.'

Hugh hung down his head; he knew that to seek his own happiness was the only right thing left.

'Utterly undeserved,' he murmured.

'As to that,' said Arthur, with much feeling, 'who could deserve love like—like theirs? I felt that, thoughtless fellow as I was, always. I had done nothing. I *was* nothing much, you know. I said so once to Mysie, and she thought it over, and that last Sunday afternoon I remember she said as we walked back together, that she had been considering what I said—I'm afraid I had never thought of it again—and that she did not think any-one need trouble about not deserving the love that was given them; for did not un-deserved love lie at the very foundation of the Christian religion, yet the love of God made people happy, and we made each other happy by our love? Wasn't it a wonderful, wise thing for a girl to say? And it's true; when I think of her love, I can better bear the want of herself.'

How well Hugh recognised the sweet, well-expressed wisdom of Mysie's little sayings! It struck home with an application far deeper than Arthur guessed. Had not his whole history during the past year been one long attempt to expiate his own sin, to atone himself for his errors, to absolve his own conscience from its remorse?

He looked up, with his eyes swimming in tears, at Arthur.

' I shall go, then,' was all he said.

' That's right ; let's get on, then, and you can have a look at Bradshaw.'

Hugh laughed at this practical suggestion, and presently remembered that, as Miss Venning's holidays had begun, Violante would not be in Oxley.

'Well, you could find out her uncle's address—Jem knows it.'

'Oh, I know where he lives,' said Hugh, declining to encounter Jem. 'Come what may, I shall come back to you at once,' he said.

'Well—send me a telegram, and I could come and meet you. You know we should have gone home in a week or so, anyhow.'

Violante was alone at Signor Mattei's lodgings. Rosa's wedding was to take place in about a fortnight, and the little drawing-room was full of preparations for it. Rosa's modest trousseau, her uncle's gift, looked magnificent lying on the chairs and sofa, where her cousins had been inspecting it before taking her out to make further purchases. It was a hot, sunny afternoon, and Violante, as she stood in the window, thought how dusty the trees looked in the little garden, how brown the grass, and how shabby altogether was the aspect of London in

August. For almost the first time she thought, with a faint sense of regret, of Civita Bella, with its harmonious colours, its fretted spires, the deep blue of the skies, the flowers. She glanced at Rosa's white bridal wreath, just sent home, and took it up in her hand—orange flowers, myrtle, and stephanotis, but these were dry and false; those other blossoms—— Violante heard a little noise, she turned her head, and there stood Hugh Crichton, tall and stately, just as he had come towards her over the old palace floor more than a year ago. She was so utterly surprised, and yet his presence fitted in so justly with her thoughts that she stood waiting, with her eyes on his face, without one conventional word of greeting. Hugh had rehearsed a thousand greetings; what he uttered was a new one—

'Violante—Violante! will you forgive me?—can you love me still?'

He held out both hands imploringly.

Violante looked up in his face; she dropped
the wreath, and in a moment, neither knew
how, he held her in his arms, and the long
year of parting was a year that was past.
He had come back; what had she to do with
mistrust or pride?

'My darling—oh, my darling! I have
not been so faithless as I seemed,' he said.
'I was misled, and then——'

'I never broke my promise,' sobbed
Violante; 'before you were gone I threw
the diamonds away. I was never engaged
to him—never.'

'It was all my own wrong-headed folly
and suspicion. And then, you know our
terrible story?'

'I know many things now,' said Violante,
withdrawing a little. 'Mr. Crichton, I have
seen your home, and I know the difference
between us. I have not wondered lately
that you did not come back.'

'Never think of that,' cried Hugh, 'for

my life is worth nothing without you. I have been so miserable that I could lead no life at all. Oh, my darling, give yourself back to me, and I will—I will be good to you! I will make you happy. I have loved you every moment of this bitter year. Oh, make the rest of my life better!'

So Hugh pleaded, with all that past bitterness giving force to his words. And she, who needed no urging, whose love had been his without an hour's wavering, felt all her troubles floating away, till the dusty suburban drawing-room was filled with a sunlight as glorious as the Italian palace, and there needed no scent of southern flowers to bring back the charm of their one half-hour of happiness. It had come back to them, and by the long want of it they knew far better what it was worth.

CHAPTER XLIII.

THE LESSON OF. LOVE.

'Wed a maiden of your people,'
Warning said the old Nokomis;
'Go not eastward, go not westward,
For a stranger whom we know not!
Like a fire upon the hearth-stone
To a neighbour's homely daughter;
Like the starlight or the moonlight
Is the handsomest of strangers!'
Thus dissuading spake Nokomis,
And my Hiawatha answered
Only this: 'Dear old Nokomis,
Very pleasant is the firelight,
But I like the starlight better,
Better do I like the moonlight.'

WHEN Rosa came in from her shopping the
first sight her eyes beheld was her white
wreath on the floor, but before she could
speak Violante sprang into her arms.

'Rosina, oh, Rosina! who do you think is here?'

As Hugh's tall figure appeared in the background Rosa had not much difficulty in answering this question; but the look in her bright, straightforward eyes was not wholly a welcome, though she held out her hand as he took Violante's and said:

'You will give her to me now?'

'Mr. Crichton,' said Rosa, 'my little sister has no mother, and my father is not accustomed to English ways. You will forgive me if I ask you a few questions. She has already suffered a great deal from suspense.'

'You can ask no questions that I am not ready to answer fully,' said Hugh.

Rosa kissed Violante, and sent her upstairs, with a decision that admitted of no question. Then she picked up her wreath, and asked Hugh to sit down, while he forestalled her by saying:

'Miss Mattei, you are aware of the misunderstanding under which I left Civita Bella,
and of the repulse I received from your
father? I hope he will give me a different
answer now.'

'Indeed, Mr. Crichton, there have been a
great many misunderstandings. Is it only
now that you have discovered your mistake?'

'No, Miss Mattei,' said Hugh, colouring,
'it is some weeks since I have felt certain
that I was mistaken. But if you know in
how much trouble we have been during the
past year—and—and my share in it, you will,
perhaps, understand that it was my cousin
Arthur's discovery of my secret and his
encouragement which has made me venture
here now.'

Rosa was softened.

'Ah, yes, Violante told me,' she said.

'I could not have raised any discussion
about myself at such a time. I don't think
you like protestations, Miss Mattei, but I

think a year is long enough to test our constancy, and surely—surely, Signor Mattei's objections can no longer exist.'

'No, she must choose for herself now. Mr. Crichton, I'm afraid I am very ungracious,' said Rosa warmly; ' but I have been so anxious for Violante. I know this will be best for her, if—if nothing *now* comes in the way.'

' Nothing can—nothing *shall.*' And Signor Mattei ? '

' I think, Mr. Crichton, that it would be a good thing if you spoke first to my uncle, Mr. Grey. He has shown Violante and myself so much kindness that we feel he ought to be consulted. You would find him at home, he is not much engaged at this time of year—and—and—life has taken a very different turn for my little sister from anything that we anticipated for her. You will not forget that you are going to take her into a strange world ? '

Rosa's eyes filled with tears as she looked earnestly at Hugh.

'I will try,' said Hugh simply, but something in his tone impressed Rosa, who saw him depart in search of Mr. Grey with more satisfaction than she could have imagined possible. Hugh found himself obliged to make a very clear statement of his circumstances, his independence of his mother, and the home at the Bank House, to which he would bring Violante, in all which matters he acquitted himself to Mr. Grey's satisfaction; his own manner and appearance probably being strong arguments in his favour. Nor, of course, could Mr. Grey be insensible to the advantage of such a provision for the girl who had failed once in her attempt to earn her living and might easily fail again. He concluded with—

'Well, Mr. Crichton, you must not suppose that I am not aware of how good a prospect you offer to my niece; but I hope you have considered well your own feelings. Violante is as sweet a girl as any man could wish to see. Her father is a gentleman born, and I don't do you the injustice to suppose that you will make yourself unhappy about the accident of her former profession any more than you have about her want of fortune. But she is to all intents and purposes a foreigner, she has none of the training, and probably few of the ideas of an ordinary English girl; do not be disappointed ˉ when you find this out.'

'Do you suppose I wish her to be like an ordinary English girl?' exclaimed Hugh.

'No,' said Mr. Grey, shrewdly; 'but, having chosen your humming-bird, don't expect her to turn out a robin redbreast.'

'I am not so unreasonable,' began Hugh; then changing his tone, 'You judge me rightly if you think I am apt to be harsh and stern, but if I can be gentle to anyone it is

to her. I could not wish her other than she
is for a moment.'

In the meantime Rosa had prepared Signor Mattei's mind for what was coming. He
listened to her with tolerable patience, looked
ruefully round the room at her wedding pre-
sents, and said :

' Was not one enough ? '

' We couldn't well help its happening at
the same time, you see, father. And I always
felt that there was a great risk that Violante
would not be strong enough even for the
concerts. I hope you will not oppose her
happiness.'

' No, figlia mia, no ; my time of opposition is over. My children do not love my
art, and are grown beyond me. You are
English, rich, respectable; the life of the
artist is not for you.'

' Oh, father ! ' cried Violante, bursting into
a flood of tears. ' Indeed, it is not so ; I am
not rich, I am not respectable, only I love

him so, father, just as you love music, how can I help it? That is all.'

'Ah, well, you are your mother's daughters. Perhaps I may hand down to my grandchildren my own ambitions!'

With which distant, and, perhaps, doubt-fully-desirable probability, Signor Mattei was forced to content himself; but there was enough truth in his disappointment to make a piece of good-fortune that now befell him very delightful to his daughters.

He had been so much separated from his own family that their existence was hardly realised by his children; but about this time he received a letter from Milan, saying that an uncle, his father's last surviving brother, who had been a physician, had died at an advanced age, and had left him a small com-petence. He was thus set free from the necessity of seeking engagements which would grow more precarious as he grew older, and could set to work to compose his

long-dreamed-of opera in any place which
he preferred.

'My children,' he said, when the first
surprise was over, ' you can live without me,
and, doubtless, the gentlemen you are about
to marry can do so too.   Your England'
(this form of expression always distressed
Violante) 'is a great country to visit, but I
am Italian.   I shall go and visit the tomb
of my honoured uncle at Milan, and then,
perhaps, at Civita Bella old Maddalena and
I can lead a quiet life together.   She knows
my ways.'

'And when we come to see you, father,'
whispered Violante, ' will you not give me
the old china bowl?'

Before, however, things had arrived at
this satisfactory condition many other arrangements had been made.   Mrs. Crichton
had been at the sea and was on the point of
coming to London, on her way back to
Redhurst, for a final inspection of Jem's ar-

rangements ; and, Hugh's scruples at shorten-
ing Arthur's stay in Wales giving way to the
desire for so powerful an ally, he asked him
to come to London and join him there.
Arthur did so, and found that Hugh had
already sought out James, who was tied to
his work, in view of the lengthened holiday
he meant to take in September, and had informed him of the state of the case. James
was quite ready at last to accept the necessity, but revenged himself by giving Arthur
the ludicrous side of the old courting time,
and enjoying a hearty laugh over Hugh's
secret.

So, to Mrs. Crichton's great surprise, she
was met at her hotel, not by James with
his hands full of patterns, but by her eldest
son, looking so grave that her first words
were :

'My dear Hugh, what brings you here?
Is anything the matter ? '

'No, mother, nothing ; but Arthur and I

are in town, and I wanted to say a few words
to you.'

Frederica was staying with a school-
friend, so Mrs. Crichton was alone ; and Hugh
hurried her over her cup of tea, and was
unusually attentive and unusually impatient
till she had finished with her maid and her
orders to the hotel people, and could give her
mind to his story, into the midst of which he
plunged, hurrying through it with tolerable
candour, and at last breaking off abruptly
and waiting for his mother's reply.

She was taken exceedingly by surprise,
and though she was a woman of many words
at first she hardly said anything. She was
honestly desirous that her son should marry,
and did not stand in that sort of relation to
him which his marriage would disturb, and
she was clear-sighted enough at once to re-
cognise that this was no fancy which could
be talked away.

'Mother, why don't you speak to me?' said Hugh.

'I hardly know what to say to you, my dear. You have surprised me exceedingly; but I do not expect that anything that I say could induce you to alter your choice.'

'But, mother, you've seen her?' said Hugh, entreatingly.

'Yes; she is very pretty, and everyone speaks well of her; and, I have no doubt what you say about her relations is correct. But, Hugh, she is an Italian.'

'Surely, that is an unworthy prejudice!'

'Not at all. She may be as good as any English girl, but she will be different. She will not like the life of an English lady. Differences will start up in an unexpected manner. I have seen a great deal of life; and I don't see how people are to be happy together with such thoroughly different antecedents. You will puzzle her, and she will disappoint you.'

'I would rather *she* disappointed me than
that anyone else should fulfil my most perfect ideal,' said Hugh, ardently.

'But, indeed, Hugh, had you none of
these doubts when you delayed so long in
carrying out your intentions?'

'I delayed,' said Hugh colouring, 'because I did not wish to raise this discussion
at a time of such trouble—because I could
not grieve Arthur.   He approves of this.'

'And you have really set your heart on
her all this year?'

'Set my heart!' exclaimed Hugh, start-
ing up.   'Mother, she was never out of my
heart all the time when my mind was full of
Arthur, when I thought renouncing her was
the only atonement I could make to him!'

'How could it affect Arthur?'

'I thought no devotion, no sacrifice
would be enough to make up to him ever so
little.   And what right have I to any happiness of my own?   Oh, I have been very

miserable ; the only softness, the only sweetness, was the thought of her !' said Hugh, vehemently.

'My dear boy,' said Mrs. Crichton, 'that view was wrong. You could not give Arthur back what he lost. I think you blame yourself unduly ; but, be that as it may, though we cannot undo the consequences of our actions, you seem to have forgotten that pardon was granted to the greatest of sinners not for any atonement that they could make, but for their repentance and love. We do not stand on our own merits—surely I need not say this to you.'

Mrs. Crichton was a woman who very rarely spoke on serious subjects, and her sons could almost count the few occasions in their lives when she had so addressed them. She rarely criticised their behaviour ; but they knew that her judgment of them was almost invariably true.

'Yes mother,' said Hugh, 'I have had need to work out that truth. But if I have in any way done so it has been through Arthur's love and forgiveness, so undeserved —so unmerited. But mother, I could not even have turned to that but for the one thing that kept my heart alive—my love for Violante. I would have taken all my happiness from her—I loved her! Though I injured her I let her forgive me!'

Hugh's speech was somewhat confused; and, perhaps, his mother only partially understood him. He was only beginning to understand himself. For his history, with its attempt at atonement, hopeless till humble love made the offering acceptable and the pardon possible, was surely like a parable of the Greatest of all Histories, of human sin and Divine love, which this deep personal experience might help him profitably to realise. But Mrs. Crichton did see that, through all this storm and conflict, the natural spontaneous love for Violante had been as a star in his heart—often obscured, indeed, by clouds of doubt and suspicion; but shining in and out till day returned. Whatever sorrow it had brought, however unwise it might be, it had kept Hugh from despair, and she could not scorn it.

'My dear,' she said, 'it is too late for me to oppose what has survived so much. Nor have I the right; at your age you must please yourself. Of course, I wish you had chosen otherwise.'

'I think you will not wish so for long,' said Hugh, as he kissed her warmly.

Mrs. Crichton was not ready to accede to this remark; she was troubled and anxious; and when Arthur presently came to see her and Hugh left him with her she expressed her doubts strongly.

'You wouldn't wish Hugh to lose his better half, Aunt Lily,' he said, half playfully, and then he told of Violante's simplicity and

sweetness till Mrs. Crichton was half convinced, though she still held to—

'Yes, my dear, it was very delightful for
you all to rave about her; but can you
imagine her Hugh's wife, and an English
lady of position?'

'Well, Aunt Lily, I can imagine Hugh
very well as her husband, which is the point
to interest you, I suppose.'

Mrs. Crichton behaved beautifully. She
forestalled Hugh's proposals for an introduction, by going with him the next day to call
on Violante, who was now staying with the
Greys, from whose house Rosa was to be
married.

Violante was alone in the drawing-room,
and she started up flushing and trembling,
then, without heeding Hugh, she went right
up to Mrs. Crichton and put her little hand
in hers.

'I will try so hard to please you, Signora,'
she said, with faltering lips.

' My dear, I am not difficult to please,' said Mrs. Crichton, and somehow her fears of incongruity and incompleteness went into the background before the charm of the soft eyes and the sweet humility of the heroine of her son's romance, which, for good or for evil, was to be the one great reality of his life.

CHAPTER XLIV.

THE LESSON OF LIFE.

'His days with others will the sweeter be
For those brief days he spent in loving me.'

TOWARDS the end of August Florence
Venning returned from a visit to her brother,
eager, of course, to hear the details of the
wonderful event that had taken place during
her absence. Her sisters, however, had not
much to tell her, as Mrs. Crichton had only
just returned to Redhurst. Hugh had been
perforce busy since he came back, and
Arthur had remained for some little time
with Jem. They were all at home now,
however, and Flossy set off on the afternoon

after her return to call on Mrs. Crichton and hear the news, with which Oxley was ringing from head-quarters. As she walked along the road she was overtaken by Arthur, who greeted her cordially.

'I am so glad I have met you,' he said; 'I have a great deal to tell you, and it is a very long time since we had the chance of a conversation.'

'Yes,' said Flossy. 'I never was so astonished, *never!* Latterly, I had half fancied that Violante had some one on her mind; but that it should be Hugh!'

'No one ever suspected him of such a romance, did they? However, it is all turning out very well, and Aunt Lily likes her very much.'

'I suppose she won't come back to school?'

'Well, no, I think under the circumstances that would hardly answer. But she, with Mr. and Mrs. Fairfax—you know her

sister was married last week—are to come
and pay us a visit; so you will soon see
Violante, and, no doubt, she will tell you all
her little secrets.'

'I shall be so glad to see her. We shall
miss her very much—she is as good and
sweet as she is pretty. When——?'

'When are they going to be married, do
you mean?—I think in October.'

'That is very soon,' said Flossy.

'Yes, but there are reasons. Her father
is going to live in Italy, at Civita Bella, and
Hugh thinks he will take her there once
more. And besides—I have something to
tell you, Flossy, about myself.'

Flossy looked up at him, struck by the
grave tone. He looked quite well, and had
lost his air of languor and preoccupation;
but his manner was serious, though now he
looked in her face and smiled.

'Well, it is a long story, and I think you
will be surprised. I can't tell you how

thoughtful Hugh has been for me through all this, and he *knows* I have come to a right decision, though he does not like it.'

Flossy still looked at him, unable to frame a question, and he went on :

' Perhaps you don't know that our Bank has a sort of branch in Calcutta, not absolutely in connection with this one, but belonging to a cousin of my father's. Our grandfather, I believe, owned them both. Hugh had a letter last week from this cousin, saying that his son, who has been educated in England—I don't know if you remember him—Walter Spencer—he spent Christmas with us once—had found, on coming out, that India did not suit his health, and had to throw up the good opening out there. He is a very clever fellow, I believe ; and, though his father did not exactly say so, I think he hoped that Hugh would make some proposal to him. He offers his vacant place to me, or to George, if I was otherwise provided for—you see he knows nothing of the circumstances.'

Arthur had made many pauses during this long speech ; but Flossy did not answer him a word. She turned deadly pale, and there was an expression in her large blue eyes as she resolutely returned his enquiring looks so miserable that he could not forget it. He could not but see that his words affected her very strongly.

'You are going, then?' she said, at length.

'Yes,' said Arthur, 'I have made up my mind to go. I should like to tell you all my reasons, because, Flossy, you have always listened to my troubles, and I know how you grieved with me as well as for me.'

'Oh, yes—yes!' faltered Flossy, thankful for the tears that seemed to bring her senses back, and for this excuse for them.

'The idea made Hugh wretched,' said

Arthur, 'but yet he knew there was a great deal of sense in it. He knows that *here* everything brings back what's lost. I cannot bear it. I *cannot* forget what I hoped my life would be. The best would be a sort of make-shift. But my life is before me, and I *must* not look on it as only fit to throw away. I *must* make something of it yet, if I can. And as for the parting with them all, that's the lot of hundreds. I have fewer ties than most.'

'It is such an ending, Arthur!' said Flossy, sadly.

'No. I hope it will be a beginning— with God's help. You told me once that *she* would have made a life for herself without *me*. I don't think she would wish mine to have no future.'

'And has Hugh consented?'

'Yes. You know he said at first that I made a mistake in coming home; but that is not so. Last winter I could not have decided on such a step as this. And now he has made me promise that I will give it up if I am ill, or if I dislike it very much. But the first is not likely to happen, and the second—shall not.'

'But what does Mrs. Crichton say?' asked Flossy.

'Oh, they are all very sorry, Flossy, and so am I,' said Arthur, with an odd sort of smile, 'but—they'll get on very well without me, and I must make my way for myself as others do. I cannot be the worse,' he added, in a lower tone, 'for—for *her* memory.'

Flossy walked on in silence—it was almost more than she could bear. She hardly knew which was the saddest—that no one seemed to depend on Arthur for happiness, or that he seemed to regret their independence so little.

'What shall *I* do?' was in her heart,

and she was speechless, lest it should find its way to her tongue.

'You know, Flossy,' he said, after a pause, 'a sorrow like mine swallows up everything. I can't care very much for lesser partings. Don't think me heartless. I shall never forget any of you; but things are so changed that, now that I have partly got over the shock, I feel as if an outward change were only the natural consequence of the inner one.'

It was natural enough. Arthur had had many affections, but only one love. There had always been a sort of self-reliance about him; while he had taken gratefully all the sympathy and all the tenderness that was offered him he had never been able to depend on any of it. There was a great risk of hardening; but he had the safeguards of an unselfish disposition, the pure and perfect love that could not die with its object, and a most earnest desire not to fall short of what

Mysie's betrothed had hoped to be. He would try hard to hold himself upright, and it might be trusted that, with the blessing of the prayers of those who loved him, he might realise a yet higher love than Mysie's, and keep his heart soft and open for the days when even another earthly love might come to fill it. There was no thought of such a time in the heart of the poor girl by his side, who endured, not, indeed, the most passionate, or the most keen, but, perhaps, the most depressing grief a woman can know. But Flossy was young and bright and strong; and, moreover, the passion that only an idealistic nature could have entertained needed very little nourishment, and could find some satisfaction in imagination, admiration, and just the spark of possibility that would not define itself into hope.

In other words, so long as Flossy knew that Arthur's life was all she could wish it to be, she would lead her own, *having no closer*

ties to remember, without intolerable disturbance or dissatisfaction. It would not spoil
all other interests, because the world held
for her an interest surpassing them all.

But the last days were very hard to
endure ; and, though the impulsive outspoken girl guarded every word and look,
though Arthur parted from her as from
a sister, there came a day when the new
depths in her clear, honest eyes, the new
tones in her fresh, firm voice, came back on
his recollection and suggested a new ending
to her story.

To Hugh, in the midst of his own happiness, and such happiness as he had never
imagined for himself, it was a great pang to
find that Arthur must seek content without
his help, and find it away from his side.
His judgment acquiesced, and, perhaps,
nothing showed how well he had learnt his
late hard lessons as the way in which he

made everything easy, and secured for his cousin the lot that he had chosen as best for himself.

So Arthur went forth from among them whither these pages cannot follow him, as his young energies recovered their force, and a new life gradually roused his old interest in new hopes and new ambitions.

At home the old canal gave place to the new railroad, and the wedding parties no longer drank tea at the 'Pot of Lilies;' but rushed over it and beyond it to more distant and exciting places of entertainment, before the old rector and his wife entered into the promise of their golden wedding, after the fifty years that 'were such a little bit of eternity.'

A new generation of girls, among whom Emily Tollemache was for a short time numbered, found Miss Florence still bright and enthusiastic, Miss Clarissa full of her little nephews, while, away in London, Rosa Fairfax congratulated herself that teaching was over for her for ever. Signor Mattei, in sunny Italy, dreamed over and composed the opera that was to be more famous than his daughter's voice ; while the precious china bowl held the place of honour in the Bank House drawing-room, and was discovered by Jem to be quite in the highest style of art, and worth *anything* to a collector.

'People find things out in time,' said Hugh, with a smile, as his romantic choice was justified by the real happiness that resulted from it. For Violante was all that Hugh needed, and what more could she need herself? His love and his happiness made her own.

But there never came a day that Hugh forgot to look for Arthur's letters, or to feel responsible for his fortunes ; never a day when the incompleteness of Arthur's life did not mar the perfection of his own. Nor ever will, till, amid the scenes of the sorrow that closed his youth, Arthur finds the happiness of his manhood.

THE END.

LONDON : PRINTED BY
SPOTTISWOODE AND CO., NEW-STREET SQUARE
AND PARLIAMENT STREET

www.ingramcontent.com/pod-product-compliance
Lightning Source LLC
Chambersburg PA
CBHW030355270326
41926CB00009B/1117

* 9 7 8 3 3 3 7 3 4 5 4 3 3 *